"At Vistage, we've seen time and again that the most profound leadership transformations don't happen in isolation—they happen in community. That's what makes *The Leadership Journeyman* so powerful. Peter Schwartz, an award-winning Vistage Chair, captures the essence of what makes peer groups extraordinary: the courage to be real, the wisdom of shared experience, and the growth that only comes when leaders are willing to challenge—and be challenged.

This isn't just a book about leadership skills. It's about the deep, inner and outer work of becoming a more conscious, integrated, and effective leader. Drawing on the most current research, the insights of adult development theory, and over twenty years leading CEO peer advisory groups, Peter Schwartz shows us that true leadership is as much about who we are becoming as it is about what we are achieving.

For anyone who has ever sat at a peer group table and felt the spark of transformation, this book puts language to that experience—and expands it into a journey. It's a must read for leaders who want to walk that path with greater clarity, authenticity, and purpose."

—Sam Reese, CEO, Vistage Worldwide

"In *The Leadership Journeyman*, CEO coach Peter Schwartz intertwines wisdom from two decades of executive leadership coaching with the transformative lessons he encountered on his pilgrimage on the Camino de Santiago. Drawing powerful parallels between leadership and pilgrimage, Schwartz challenges readers to embrace imperfection, let go of outdated success strategies, and evolve into more authentic, adaptive leaders. A must read for current and future leaders, this book is both a mirror and a map for navigating the complexities of leadership with clarity, courage, and heart."

—Gordon J. Bernhardt, CFP®, Strategic Advisor, Principal at Modera Wealth Management, LLC

"This book reflects the very journey our executive team took with Peter, grounded in The Leadership Circle 360, deepened by Vistage peer group insight, and guided by the kind of clarity that only comes through real reflection. Like the Camino, it's not a quick fix—it's a path. And for leaders ready to walk it, this book is the perfect guide."

—David W. Pijor, Chairman and CEO, FVCBank

"Peter Schwartz accompanies you through *The Leadership Journeyman* as he has done in person with hundreds of executives on their leadership walk. Intertwined with his personal story of transformation along the Camino de Santiago, he marks the path with practical tools and insights. I found myself enjoying, absorbing, and sinking into its richness as I walked slowly through this book, versus a race to the end."

—Deborah Fell, Managing Partner, Chief Outsiders

"Peter Schwartz combines his leadership experience, his CEO coaching abilities, and his personal touch with the incredible journey of walking the Camino De Santiago to highlight all the analogies of everyday life and the leadership journey he helps so many different people take. Peter has been instrumental in my leadership develop-ment as I continue to quote or reference guidance he has provided. *The Leadership Journeyman* is an excellent way to absorb a career's worth of experience in just one book."

—Matthew Dean, Managing Partner, Scare the Bear Capital

"Pete has been my coach for fifteen years. During that time, he's helped me navigate multiple economic crises and a pandemic; he's helped me define my leadership values; and he's held me accountable as my company created new services and grew. With *The Leader-ship Journeyman*, you won't need coaching for a decade to gain Pete's wisdom, guidance, and insights. You'll appreciate what I call Pete-isms, and find his advice practical and highly effective. I wish you good luck in your business and leadership journey."

—Joanna Pineda, Founder, CEO, and Chief Troublemaker,
Matrix Group International, Inc.

"We all aspire to live a life of purpose and impact. This book provides the framework for each of us to reach higher. I will be a better leader because of it, and so will you."

—Todd Hauptli, CEO, American Association of Airport Executives

THE

LEADERSHIP
JOURNEYMAN

THE
LEADERSHIP
JOURNEYMAN

INSIGHTS FROM A CEO COACH
ON LIFELONG GROWTH, MEANING, AND PURPOSE
FROM THE CAMINO DE SANTIAGO

PETER D. SCHWARTZ

Entrepreneur | Books

Copyright © 2026 by Peter D. Schwartz.

All rights reserved. No part of this book may be used or reproduced in any manner whatsoever without prior written consent of the author, except as provided by the United States of America copyright law.

Published by Entrepreneur® Books, Charleston, South Carolina.
An imprint of Advantage Media Group.

Entrepreneur® Books is a registered trademark of Entrepreneur Media, LLC and used under license to Advantage Media Group.

Printed in the United States of America.

10 9 8 7 6 5 4 3 2 1

ISBN: 979-8-89701-038-7 (Paperback)
ISBN: 979-8-89701-039-4 (eBook)

Library of Congress Control Number: 2025921196

Cover design by Matthew Morse.
Layout design by Lance Buckley.

This custom publication is intended to provide accurate information and the opinions of the author in regard to the subject matter covered. It is sold with the understanding that the publisher, Entrepreneur® Books, is not engaged in rendering legal, financial, or professional services of any kind. If legal advice or other expert assistance is required, the reader is advised to seek the services of a competent professional.

Since 1977, Entrepreneur Media has been dedicated to inspiring, informing, and celebrating the innovators who drive business forward. Entrepreneur® Books, launched in 2024 through a partnership with Entrepreneur Media, continues that mission by helping business and thought leaders share their insights, experiences, and expertise through custom books. Opinions expressed by authors of Entrepreneur® Books are their own. To be considered for publication, please visit books.Entrepreneur.com.

To my wife, Elaine, and son, Peter

CONTENTS

THE LEADERSHIP JOURNEYMAN

> *Life shrinks or expands in proportion to one's courage.*

—ANAÏS NIN

I stood at the Cruz de Ferro, the Iron Cross that marks one of the highest points of the Camino de Santiago, almost five thousand feet up Monte Irago. Like countless pilgrims before me, I had carried a rock in my backpack, meant to symbolize a burden, from the start of my journey. Now was the moment to let it go. After placing my rock among the thousands of others at the base of the cross, I made my way down the mountain, my arthritic knees protesting every step.

By the time I reached the pilgrim hotel, I was exhausted and in pain. I took a shower, and as I headed toward my bed, I caught a glimpse of my face in the mirror. What I saw shocked me. It was an aging, worn-out, tired, old man's face. It was my father's face.

That was my Camino moment.

That day in the summer of 2015, I was one of approximately 219,000 people who walk the French Way, or Camino Francés, the most popular route of the Camino de Santiago, every year. They follow the nearly five-hundred-mile path traveled by pilgrims since medieval times to reach the shrine of Saint James the Apostle, in the Spanish town of Santiago de Compostela. Some come seeking a spiritual experience, some for self-discovery, some for a once-in-a-lifetime adventure.

That summer, the summer I turned sixty-two, I was seeking all of the above, with an emphasis on the first two. For over a month, I was not Peter Schwartz but simply *peregrino*, or pilgrim in Spanish, which is what the locals called me. I loved the anonymity of the name, of being one among thousands, all of us with our backpacks and hiking boots. It felt freeing to leave my normal life behind and join this community of fellow travelers from all over the world.

By the time I climbed Monte Irago, I had been walking for twenty-two days, taking in the ancient churches and Roman roads, shaped and softened by centuries of weather and time—a living embodiment of the Japanese aesthetic of *wabi-sabi*, which embraces the beauty in imperfection and impermanence.

Still, that experience had not quite prepared me for the shock of seeing what time had done to my own face.

"Get yourself back in front of the mirror," I said to myself. "Stand there and look at the face and the person behind the face. And get good with the fact that you are not permanent, you are not perfect, and you are not complete."

It was a hell of a moment.

The next day, as I was doing my walking, about two hours in, I realized something had changed for me. It wasn't a thunderbolt moment in front of the mirror; it was the culmination of a journey. I finally understood that I had to let go of this need to be perfect, be permanent, be complete. It had been my lifelong strategy to do all those things, but now all I wanted was to simply grow and to be in the present moment on the Camino.

Which has turned out to be an excellent metaphor for leadership development.

My name is Peter Schwartz, and leadership development is my profession. For twenty years, I have served as a Vistage Chair, leading exclusive peer advisory groups of CEOs and senior executives in this elite global leadership organization. In this role, I lead CEO forums, guiding confidential discussions around members' most difficult challenges. In addition, I provide high-level executive coaching to help accomplished leaders sharpen their decision-making, elevate their leadership, and drive exceptional business results.

I've worked with 379 CEOs at the time of writing this, and I've seen extraordinary things happen, such as businesses growing from five million in annual revenue to one hundred million in annual revenue, day after day after day. That's the power of the peer group, but it's also about the leader's approach and vision. As a leader, I believe my role in leadership development goes deeper than strategy or skills; it's about helping to direct spirit, or life energy—although I wouldn't frame it that way directly to anyone I'm coaching, as "spirit" might sound a little too "woo-woo" for the average CEO searching for the secret to exponential growth.

What I do tell them is that we come into our adult lives having formulated a specific success strategy. And because it works, we want to perfect it, we want to make it permanent, and we want to feel complete in it. We become identified with our success strategies and, as a result, we develop habits of thinking and patterns of behaving.

But the moment you're promoted into leadership, that construction starts to crumble. Leadership demands that we let go of fixed ideas of ourselves and our roles and continue to strive to grow ever better, constantly expanding our capacities. This is the real point of the leadership journey: to recognize that nothing is permanent, perfect, or complete.

To me, this commitment to ongoing growth is what it means to be a leadership journeyman as opposed to, say, a leadership master. The term *journeyman* comes from the old trades and refers to someone who's completed an apprenticeship but is still on the path, still refining. Still learning.

To be a journeyman, by definition, means to be in the midst of a journey, growing your capacity to address a range of complexity. In leadership, that complexity never ends—there is always something new, adaptive, and emergent that the leader has never seen before. The term *master* indicates the highest level of proficiency, but how can a leader be proficient in something they've never seen, done, or encountered?

Like the Camino, leadership is a path that must be taken step-by-step, with each experience deepening our understanding and revealing new challenges. Great leaders learn not to cling to a finished version of themselves but to stay open to change, continually growing and adapting their ability to lead in whatever moment they face.

That's why I wrote this book—to share what I've learned about this journey, both from my own experiences and from working with so many leaders navigating the same path. This book is an invitation to embrace this journey of leadership, to let go of the need for perfection and embrace the power of ongoing growth.

For the most part, I have been someone who welcomes growth and change. I have always been a seeker, a peregrino, in my own life. I see spirituality as an identification with the Divine, and I have spent much of my life searching for ways to embrace and live fully through my aspect of divinity. This started in childhood, as I grew up outside Philadelphia in a very Catholic family, proudly served as an altar boy, and attended Catholic grammar and high schools.

But even as a teenager, I was looking for answers ... answers the priest in my sophomore religion class was unable to provide. As a form of protest, I intentionally failed the class and then embarked on my own course of spiritual study, reading about mythologies, world religions, and just about everything Joseph Campbell ever wrote.

My professional path began in a very different space. I graduated from Old Dominion University in Norfolk, Virginia, with a degree in psychology, but I did not pursue that. I went into sales—specifically technology sales—because I graduated right around the time AT&T was being deregulated, and tech was where the money was. I remained in that field for the first few decades of my career, steadily increasing my roles and responsibilities and climbing the corporate ladder.

Then I went out on my own and launched a long-distance resale company (when you could still make money doing that) and an internet start-up. It was during that phase of my career, building companies from the ground up, that I realized what I really enjoyed most was working with my team. I loved growing businesses and winning deals, but working with my team showed me that the only way in which I had 100 percent influence was in how I showed up as a leader.

I felt this stirring inside me that there was something more out there than building companies—something infinitely more interesting to me—and that was the conversation I was having and how much I was learning through developing my team. That's where I found all my energy. I made every mistake you can make as a leader and came out not discouraged but inspired, wanting to figure it out and get better at it. So, leadership became a project for me, and I became my research subject.

This all happened just as leadership coaching was emerging as a bona fide profession that could be formally studied at major universities such as Harvard and UPenn. I enrolled in Georgetown University's

Institute for Transformational Leadership, one of the pioneering programs offering a highly regarded Executive Certificate in Leadership Coaching. By taking a deep dive into leadership studies, I knew that, at the very least, I would become a better leader—or I could pivot into an entirely new career that allowed me to give 100 percent of myself to the kind of work that spoke to my soul. I studied with the same experts who were shaping this new field and came away with a vision of leadership as a journey of continuous growth and inner development and an ongoing conversation with the world around us. This resonated deeply with what I had experienced in my own leadership path and what I was witnessing in my work with executives.

When Vistage found me after I had completed my Georgetown certification, I knew I had discovered a way to put these principles into practice. I was ready to dive into the real-world demands that today's leaders face and help them grow to meet them. And I'm still doing that today, some twenty years later.

THE MODERN LEADERSHIP LANDSCAPE

Being a leader today has become increasingly challenging and unpredictable. Defined by volatility, uncertainty, complexity, and ambiguity—often summed up as "VUCA"—today's business environment demands that leaders think and act at levels beyond traditional approaches.

The most effective leaders are continually expanding their capacity to see new perspectives, handle ambiguity, and guide their teams with resilience. They are always learning and growing and pushing the boundaries of what they know. Those who fail to do so may find themselves falling into what the developmental psychologist Robert Kegan (more on him later) calls the "development gap"—the mismatch between the complexity of the environments leaders operate in and their level of internal development or self-awareness. When the demands of leadership outpace the tools a leader has to meet them, that leader must either grow or fail.

Just as the Camino de Santiago demands a willingness to be present and responsive to each day's challenges, effective leadership requires continuous adaptation and growth. Instead of focusing on a single destination, today's leaders must embrace a path of ongoing development. The Camino pilgrimage offers a perfect metaphor for this journey: Each step brings new terrain, each day demands presence and adaptability, and the path itself becomes the teacher.

Leaders, like peregrinos, must be ready to adapt to each day's challenges, remaining open to transformation through experience.

In this book, we will explore leadership development as an ongoing journey, a continuous process that aligns with my own experiences on the Camino—a path that calls for shedding old ways of thinking, embracing impermanence, and evolving to meet new challenges. Through stories, research, and lessons from my work with leaders, we'll explore the tools and insights necessary for today's leaders to grow, adapt, and thrive in this ever-shifting landscape.

At the heart of this leadership journey lie what are known in my work as the inner and outer games. The outer game encompasses the visible, measurable aspects of leadership—the skills, knowledge, and behaviors that can be observed and trained. This is where leaders are constantly honing their craft through experience, feedback, and incremental improvement.

But the inner game is where transformation truly occurs. This is the hidden dimension of self-knowledge, beliefs, and mindsets that form what's often called our "internal operating system of performance" as leaders. It's the conversation we're having with ourselves about the thing we're just about to do—the beliefs, fears, and self-talk that ultimately run the outer game. While most leaders invest heavily in their outer game, those who achieve extraordinary results must also learn to master this deeper, more challenging inner work.

I've seen this transformation unfold hundreds of times in my work with Vistage. The CEOs and senior executives I work with are already successful—they've built multimillion-dollar companies and achieved impressive results. But they recognize that in today's complex business environment, the leadership approaches that got them where they are won't take them where they want to go. That's why they've made the commitment to Vistage. They've committed to the leadership journey.

My Camino pilgrimage was a powerful catalyst for the insights and revelations that now guide my work with leaders. Throughout that five-hundred-mile trek, I kept a detailed diary, recording the photos, accounts of peak experiences, and lessons that emerged along the way. And by the time I reached the end of the French Way, four profound Camino revelations had crystallized in my mind.

CAMINO REVELATIONS

Revelation 1: Travel light. Take only what you need for the journey. Be willing to let go of everything else.

Revelation 2: Travel with *soft eyes*. Let go of the rigid and fixed images you hold for the way you think things are supposed to be and be open to the way things are. Everything that I needed to reach my final destination was there in front of me ... when I was open to seeing it.

Revelation 3: The joy is in the walking. If you are willing to do the walking, you will get the view. The destination is simply the final view.

Revelation 4: *Wabi-sabi* ... the beauty of things imperfect, impermanent, and incomplete. Over the course of this Camino, and especially after that moment in the mirror, I came to understand, accept, and embrace this Wabi-sabi view of myself.

These four revelations hold profound lessons for leaders seeking to navigate the terrain ahead. So, in the pages that follow, you will also learn to travel light by shedding the nonessential to focus on what truly matters; to travel with soft eyes that let go of fixed expectations and open you to whatever the present reality may be; to find joy in the journey itself rather than solely focusing on the ultimate destination; and, finally, to embrace your own *wabi-sabi* mindset—celebrating the beauty in imperfection, impermanence, and incompleteness, empowering you to lead with greater authenticity, adaptability, and self-acceptance.

Whether you're just starting out or seeking to deepen your impact, this book invites you to become a true leadership journeyman. Like the Camino itself, your path will call you to shed old ways of thinking, embrace change, and evolve to meet new challenges. You'll explore both the inner landscape of self-discovery and the outer terrain of practical leadership, learning to navigate them with growing wisdom and grace. Along the way, you'll develop new perspectives, challenge familiar assumptions, and discover deeper reserves of capability than you knew you possessed.

But first, before we begin our journey together, I invite you to pause for an honest self-assessment—a crucial practice that will serve you throughout your leadership career.

The QR code below will take you to my website, where you'll find instructions on how to take the free Leadership Circle self-assessment.

You might also consider these questions that will help ground you in your current reality while pointing toward your path of growth:

- What is calling you forward in your leadership role right now—what growth or change is asking to emerge?

- How have your life experiences and personal history shaped your current approach to leadership?

- As you consider the journey from expertise through achievement to impact, where do you find yourself today, and what tells you that you're ready for the next step?

Your answers may reveal both opportunities and resistance—both are natural parts of the journey. The path ahead will require an ongoing commitment to your development, a willingness to face challenges head-on, and the courage to keep learning even when it's uncomfortable. But the rewards—deeper self-awareness, more meaningful relationships, and the ability to create a lasting positive impact—make every step worthwhile.

I will be right beside you the whole way, walking with you as your fellow peregrino, offering not a rigid itinerary but a trusted guide for your own transformative journey ahead.

CHAPTER 1

PACKING YOUR BACKPACK—ESSENTIAL LEADERSHIP TOOLS

> *The journey of the hero is about the courage to seek the depths; the image of creative rebirth; the eternal cycle of change within us; the uncanny discovery that the seeker is the mystery which the seeker seeks to know. The hero journey is a symbol that binds, in the original sense of the word, two distant ideas, the spiritual quest of the ancients with the modern search for identity, always the one, shape-shifting yet marvelously constant story that we find.*
>
> **—JOSEPH CAMPBELL,** *THE HERO'S JOURNEY: JOSEPH CAMPBELL ON HIS LIFE AND WORK*

E very journey begins with preparation. Whether it's planning a cross-country road trip, training for a marathon, or embarking on the pilgrimage of a lifetime, the care and intentionality we bring to getting ready can make all the difference in our ultimate experience and success.

This was especially true for my Camino de Santiago journey. In the months leading up to my departure for Spain, I meticulously researched the nearly five-hundred-mile route, consulted guidebooks, and spoke with veteran pilgrims. Over and over, I heard the same message: "Travel light." Whatever I decided to take in my backpack with me would be something I had to carry for thirty-five days—meaning everything I needed to be able to walk across Spain had to be in that bag, and not one thing extra.

Through my research, I determined that I needed to keep my backpack under twenty-four pounds. Then I mapped out in my mind exactly what I needed to put in it. Two pairs of socks, two pairs of underwear, two essential day-to-day outfits, a raincoat, a guide-book, and a compass. I also made sure to have a pair of high-quality walking shoes that I spent the weeks before my departure thoroughly breaking in, knowing that blisters would be an unavoidable reality on the Camino.

The same level of intention I put into curating my backpack can also apply to the leadership journey. In the same way that I had to be ruthlessly discerning about what supplies I could bring to Spain, the best leaders know they must prepare for their journey by equipping themselves with the right tools and capabilities in advance, carefully choosing what to carry and what to leave behind. The weight of leadership, like a physical burden, can be a lot lighter when you've put time and thought into preparing for whatever may lie ahead—including the unexpected.

CHOOSING YOUR GUIDES: THE WISDOM THAT SHAPES OUR JOURNEY

The most essential thing we pack for any meaningful journey isn't a physical item at all—it's the wisdom of those who have walked the path before us. Just as I consulted veteran pilgrims before setting out on the Camino, choosing the right guides for the journey will shape everything that follows. And when you're preparing for a leadership journey, there are a lot of potential guides to choose from. If you look at my bookshelf, I probably have a hundred books on leadership and management by all the experts out there. While many provide valuable insights, time and again, I've turned to the same handful of guides that have most profoundly shaped my leadership journey through their wisdom.

Think of it this way: On the Camino, you might meet dozens of fellow pilgrims each day, gaining small insights from each conversation. But it's the people you choose to walk alongside for days at a time who truly shape your experience. These are the people who shaped mine and who accompanied me on both my leadership Camino and my walk, at least metaphorically, through northern Spain. That is the power of a really good peer group, by the way.

My journey began at Georgetown University's Leadership Coaching Program, where, based on what I had already learned about myself as a leader, I gravitated toward studies and research that focused on transformational leadership. It was here that I first encountered the work of Harvard-based developmental psychologist Robert Kegan, who would become one of my four primary guides on my leadership journey.

Kegan's research fundamentally changed how we understand both leadership and human development. For years, conventional wisdom claimed that our cognitive development essentially stopped around age twenty-one—that once we could think abstractly, we were done growing. Kegan proved what I had sensed as I developed into a better leader: Meaningful growth and transformation can be a lifelong process.[1] He showed that adults can develop increasingly sophisticated ways of making meaning from their experiences, moving from

---

1   Robert Kegan, *The Evolving Self: Problem and Process in Human Development* (Harvard University Press, 1982).

simply following external rules and expectations to creating their own framework for understanding the world. These insights resonated with me to the point where I spent weeks in residence in Boston, studying directly with Kegan and his coauthor and frequent collaborator, Lisa Leahy. They have had a profound influence on my work.

Around this same time, I discovered the poet and philosopher David Whyte. At first glance, he might seem like an unlikely leadership guide—who expects a poet to offer meaningful insight into organizational life? Yet, Whyte's unique perspective that life is basically an ongoing conversation with the world around us has deeply influenced my approach to leadership. He looks at what it means to lead through a completely different lens—a holistic, artistic lens that bridges what most business leaders keep separate: logic and intuition, analysis and inspiration, head and heart.[2]

Through his workshops and his approach to organizational life through poetry and storytelling, Whyte has helped me understand that leadership requires not just technical competencies but active engagement in a dynamic conversation between ourselves, our teams, and the larger world.

Bob Anderson and Bill Adams, cofounders of the Leadership Circle that I mentioned in the introduction, have also been essential guides in helping me understand the fundamental tension every leader faces: the pull between *creative* leadership driven by vision and purpose and *reactive* tendencies rooted in deep-seated insecurities.[3] Like my deep dive with Kegan, I spent time with them studying their methodology. Their insights helped me understand why some leaders remain stuck in old patterns while others forge ahead on their

---

2   David Whyte, *The Heart Aroused: Poetry and the Preservation of the Soul in Corporate America* (Currency Doubleday, 1994).

3   Robert Anderson and William Adams, *Mastering Leadership: An Integrated Framework for Breakthrough Performance and Extraordinary Business Results* (Wiley, 2015).

development journey. We will explore their highly regarded Leadership Circle Profile, a 360-degree assessment tool, later in this chapter.

Finally, Robert Fritz's work on structural dynamics completes this quartet of guides. While I never spent time with Fritz in person as I did with the others, I immersed myself in his writings, absorbing his insights about how leaders can consciously shape the underlying structures of their organizations to achieve meaningful change[4]— much like how the ancient paths of the Camino have shaped pilgrims' journeys for centuries.

These four guides—coming from developmental psychology, poetry, leadership coaching, and creative theory—illuminated different aspects of the same truth: that leadership, like a pilgrimage, is a journey of continuous growth and inner development and an ongoing conversation with the world around us. Their perspectives complemented my lifelong study of Joseph Campbell and his hero's journey—that universal pattern of transformation that occurs in every culture and across every age. While Campbell provided the archetypal map of how humans navigate and are shaped by profound change, these four guides offered practical approaches for applying these timeless principles to modern leadership.

So, just as a pilgrim might read dozens of Camino guides but choose to walk with only a few trusted companions, I've chosen to walk with these thinkers, literally in some cases, metaphorically in others. Their combined wisdom has not only informed my own journey but has proved invaluable in my work with CEOs over the past two decades, and I trust it will be helpful in your journey as well.

---

4   Robert Fritz, *The Path of Least Resistance: Learning to Become the Creative Force in Your Own Life* (Fawcett Columbine, 1989).

THE THREE PHASES OF THE LEADERSHIP JOURNEY

Of all the tools these guides have shared with me, perhaps the most valuable is their collective framework for understanding the leadership journey itself. These thinkers helped me recognize the three distinct stages that shape a leader's development—phases that, I would soon discover, were perfectly mirrored by my Camino pilgrimage.

The Physical Phase: The Journey to Expertise

During those first demanding days on the Camino, my focus was entirely physical. Despite walking twenty miles each weekend to prepare, by day four on the trail, it was brutal. But I kept walking, enduring the blisters, and gradually my body grew stronger. This physical challenge phase mirrors what Campbell described as leaving the familiar world and facing initial trials. It also aligns with Kegan's Socialized Mind stage, where leaders focus on developing fundamental capabilities, learning from authority, and meeting external standards—just as new pilgrims must learn and follow the basic rules of the Camino.

The Spiritual Phase: The Path to Achievement

After descending through the foothills into the Meseta region of Spain, the journey changed dramatically. The endless wheat fields created a different kind of challenge—one of reflection and inner work. This mirrors Campbell's period of trials and transformation, where the hero faces their inner demons. In Kegan's framework, this represents the Self-Authoring Mind stage, where leaders begin to define their own purpose and vision. Just as pilgrims in the Meseta must find their own meaning in the journey, leaders at this stage move beyond simply following established practices to create their own frameworks for understanding their role and purpose.

The Soulful Phase: The Emergence of Impact

The final phase brings integration—where the physical mastery and spiritual understanding merge into something greater. On the Camino, this is where pilgrims often discover that "the joy is in the walking." In Campbell's framework, this is the return with the elixir—where the hero brings back transformational wisdom to serve their community. Kegan describes this as the Self-Transforming Mind stage, where leaders can transcend even their own frameworks to lead with authentic presence and genuine impact.

THE TOOLS OF THE INNER GAME

In the introduction, we introduced the idea of an outer and an inner game in leadership development—the outer game being the visible skills and behaviors we can observe and train and the inner game meaning the hidden dimension of self-knowledge, beliefs, and mindsets that form our internal operating system of performance.

I can't take credit for this concept. It comes from the *Inner Game* series of books that were, at least initially, focused on sports, including *The Inner Game of Tennis* (1974)[5] and *The Inner Game of Golf* (1981)[6] by author and coach W. Timothy Gallwey. Gallwey's thesis was that athletes (and others) could improve their performance by mastering the mental aspects of personal achievement and reducing internal conflict. Bob Anderson also uses the term *internal operating system* to describe the internal frameworks we use to navigate the world.

This system begins with something we've all packed for our journey, whether we realize it or not—the success strategy I mentioned in the introduction. In fact, our internal operating system of

---

5   Timothy Gallwey, *The Inner Game of Tennis* (Random House, 1974).

6   Timothy Gallwey, *The Inner Game of Golf* (Random House, 1981).

performance might be better understood as a success strategy—a collection of beliefs, mental models, and decisions formed in our younger years that we bring into our adult lives. We'll be taking a more in-depth look at success strategies in a later chapter, but for now, understand that they work something like this:

> *In order to be safe, secure, and worthwhile in this world, I need to be seen a certain way in the eyes of others.*

In our formative years, we are keen observers of our environments, making mental notes and decisions about what we encounter, both positive and negative. From that, over time, we formulate our success strategy, which we then deploy into our adult lives—particularly our professional lives. Because it works, we begin to perfect it. We want to feel complete in it and to make it permanent.

Each of the thinkers who influenced my approach has their own take on this phenomenon; it's what Kegan refers to as the "socialized mind," what Anderson calls the "reactive mind," and what Jim Collins, who wrote *Good to Great*,[7] would call "Level 3" (or "Good") leadership or our "internal operating system of performance." Whatever we happen to call it, it works so well that we not only become identified with it, but we make it our identity. We believe the following:

> *I am my strategy.*

And the strategy works. It works well, right up to the moment a leader gets promoted into a leadership role. Suddenly, that success strategy that worked so well for an individual contributor is no longer adequate to meet the demands and complexity of leadership.

---

7   Jim Collins, *Good to Great: Why Some Companies Make the Leap ... and Others Don't* (HarperBusiness, 2001).

This is the most rigorous aspect of leadership development and the most important. A new success strategy needs to emerge in the leader, what Kegan calls the "achiever mind," Anderson calls the "creative mind," and Collins calls the "Level 5," or "Great" mind.

Every leader I have ever worked with, including myself, has struggled with this.

Ken Wilber's concept of "transcend and include"[8] offers a valuable insight into how this developmental leap works. When leaders evolve from the reactive to the creative mind, they don't simply abandon their previous capabilities. Instead, they transcend their old way of seeing the world while including its most valuable aspects. This evolution allows them to operate from a more expansive, complex, and effective worldview while retaining the useful skills and insights gained from earlier stages.

And transcendence and inclusion are crucial because, without this type of expansion, those wonderful success strategies that worked so well in a previous role will actually cancel out all the gifts the leader brings forward. That identity that the leader worked so hard to perfect, complete, and make permanent will become an identity hook—a fixed sense of self tied to those strategies—that can interfere with their leadership effectiveness in new contexts.

Understanding this inherent part of our inner game—the success strategy we all carry—helps us better appreciate the tools we consciously choose to bring on our journey. Both the map and compass are essential tools of our inner game, representing different aspects of how we understand and navigate the leadership landscape, inevitably colored by the success strategies we carry.

---

8   Ken Wilber, *A Theory of Everything: An Integral Vision for Business, Politics, Science, and Spirituality* (Shambhala Publications, 2001).

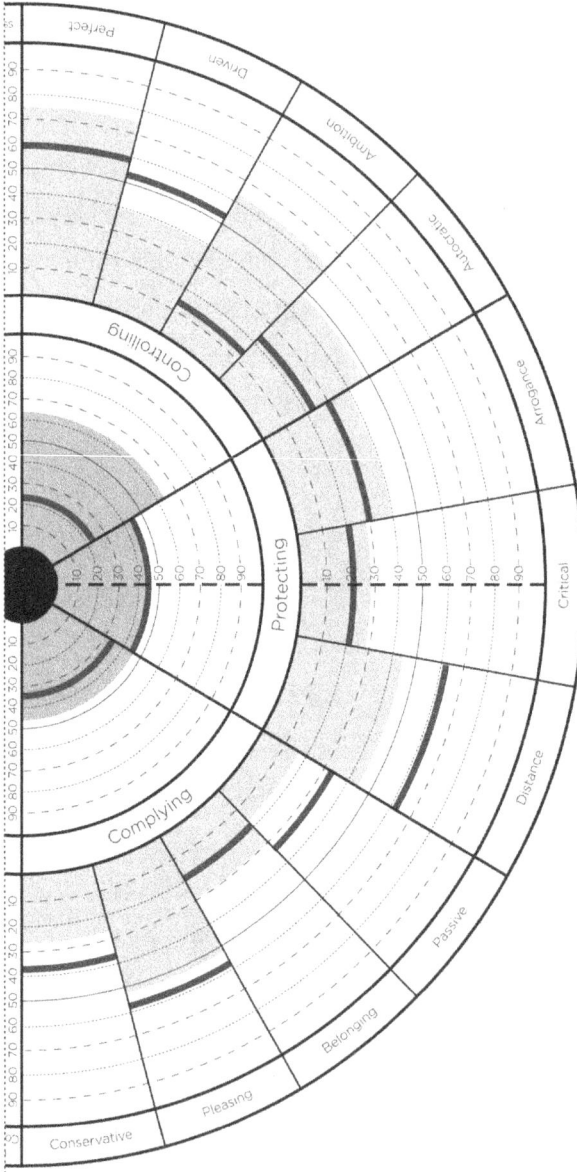

REACTIVE

Controlling Mindset:
I am my achievement

Example Identity Hooks:
- I have to deliver flawless results, or else I am a failure.
- I have to work 50 percent more than the rest or else I will not win.

Protecting Mindset:
I am my intellect

Example Identity Hooks:
- I have to know the answer or else people will think I'm stupid.
- I have to be unemotional or else I am weak.

Complying Mindset:
I am my relationship

Example Identity Hooks:
- I have the be liked or else I am not accepted.
- I have to be nice or else I don't belong.

OUR INNER MAP: MENTAL MODELS OF LEADERSHIP

The map represents our mental models of how leadership works: our understanding of authority, relationships, success, and how things get done. It's important to remember that the map is *only* a representation—neurolinguistic programming (NLP) reminds us that "the map is not the territory."

For example, picture a road map of California. The line representing Highway 1 might be a millimeter wide on the map, which, at scale, would make the actual highway half a mile wide. Of course, we all know that's not true. The line—and the map itself—is only a representation, a way of thinking about and navigating the actual road.

Similarly, our inner map of leadership is a representation of reality, not reality itself, consisting of those mental models and memories that tell us what the terrain looks like. It's made up of our deeply held images and assumptions about how leadership works—encompassing everything from what authority means to how relationships function to what success looks like. However, as with any map, it isn't reality itself, only a representation that exists to help us navigate the terrain.

I've seen the power of these mental models play out time and again in my work with leaders. One powerful example is the story of a Chinese American Vistage member I coached. This person started a government contracting business and grew it to $30 million really quickly. Then they hit the wall. There was friction with the senior leadership team, a drift when nobody was making key decisions. It was just a mess.

One day, I had this intuitive hit. "Tell me about your relationship to authority," I said. "What does authority mean to you?"

Without hesitation, this member said, "Boots on the neck."

Boots on the neck? When I asked them to unpack that, it turned out this person had been in Tiananmen Square during the Chinese student protests as a teenager. They watched as classmates were carted off and taken away, never to be seen again. Their definition of leadership became that authoritative "boots on the neck" approach, and they had made a commitment to themself that they would never, ever act like that as a leader.

Now, there's nothing wrong with that decision. However, it was a decision informed by their impoverished definition of authority—a view of the power that comes with leadership that was limited to its most negative expression, which prevented them from seeing how authority could also be used to protect, empower, and create positive change. Once that metaphor opened up, it revealed something crucial about the inner game: The words that we use matter. We each have our own definitions—our own software—and sometimes we need to upgrade those definitions.

OUR INNER COMPASS: VALUES, PURPOSE, AND DIRECTION

While our map helps us understand the territory, our inner compass helps us determine our direction. It represents our internal guidance system: our values, purpose, and the beliefs that help us determine direction. It helps us answer crucial questions: What matters most? Which path aligns with our deepest values? What feels right or wrong?

While they're essential to our leadership, our most deeply held values have the power to constrain us when we hold them too rigidly. Or, as Kegan asked, "Do you have your values, or do your values have you?"

Just as that Vistage member's impoverished definition of authority limited their leadership effectiveness, any of our core values can become similarly constrained. Take loyalty, for example. I've witnessed leaders trapped by an overly narrow view of loyalty, unable to make necessary decisions because they've turned a complex concept into a confining box.

The leadership journey requires expanding our relationship with these core values. You can be loyal to someone and still make the difficult decision to let them go because you're also being loyal to the company's mission and the rest of the team. Sometimes, the most loyal act is recognizing when a role isn't serving someone and helping them move on to better opportunities. It's not about abandoning your values but developing richer, more nuanced definitions of what matters to you to give you more freedom to lead effectively.

Similarly, I often encounter CEOs wrestling with questions of purpose, feeling like they're living a life without it. But here's a crucial insight that also comes from NLP: Purpose isn't a noun—it's not something you can go out in your yard and scoop up by the handful. Purpose is a verb. It's something you do. Just like courage isn't something you have or don't have, and loyalty is not just some static value you possess. These are active choices we make daily.

At the end of each day, you can ask yourself: *Did I act purposefully today? Did I show courage? Did I demonstrate loyalty in ways that served both individuals and the greater good?*

This shift from viewing purpose (or courage or loyalty) as something to *find* to something to *do* mirrors a broader pattern in leadership development. Remember, we all start our adult lives with that success strategy I mentioned earlier:

> In order to be safe, secure, and worthwhile in this world,
> I need to be seen a certain way in the eyes of others.

That strategy usually works, in that it gets us to where we can start the business or earn our first promotion, and there's absolutely nothing wrong with that … for a while. But the strategy has to evolve. As both Anderson and Kegan point out in their studies of adult development,[9] what becomes more important isn't playing for safety anymore—it's creating something that truly matters to us. We move from the expert mindset focused on security to something more meaningful and purpose-driven—the achievement mindset.

EMOTIONAL REGULATION: BEYOND EMOTIONAL INTELLIGENCE

One crucial aspect of the inner game is what Bob Anderson calls the "deployment of self into circumstances." This refers to our ability to bring our authentic, whole selves into the leadership situations we face, rather than hiding behind a mask or predetermined role. It's about having the self-awareness to understand our natural tendencies, triggers, and blind spots—and then consciously choose how we show up. That demands not just emotional intelligence but emotional *regulation*.

Just as we need to expand our relationship with our values and reframe our understanding of purpose, mastering our inner game requires developing a sophisticated relationship with our emotions. Or, to paraphrase Kegan again, "Do you have your emotions, or do your emotions have you?"

Consider anger, for instance. Does your anger drive the way you lead, or do you have anger and still choose how to lead? These are two very distinct leadership approaches with dramatically different impacts. Let's be clear: Anger is natural. It's human. You

---

9   Anderson and Adams, *Mastering Leadership: An Integrated Framework for Breakthrough Performance and Extraordinary Business Results*, 82.

cannot—and should not try to—leave your humanity at the door. We all get angry; it's normal. What determines your impact as a leader isn't the presence of anger but what you do when you experience it. This ability to regulate our emotional responses, rather than being regulated by them, marks a key milestone in leadership (and human) development.

Like any aspect of the inner game, this ability to regulate our emotions directly impacts how we deploy ourselves into leadership situations. When we can observe and manage our emotional responses rather than being hijacked by them, we expand our range of possible responses and become more intentional in our leadership choices.

INNER GAME TOOL: THE LEADERSHIP CIRCLE PROFILE

Earlier in this chapter, I introduced Bob Anderson and Bill Adams, whose work on creative versus reactive leadership has deeply influenced my understanding of leadership development. Now, let's explore the tool they're most known for—one that has become instrumental in my own practice: the Leadership Circle Profile.

If you have not already opted in to take the free assessment, you can do so by scanning the QR code below.

While our inner compass guides us toward what matters most, and our mental maps help us understand the terrain, we often need help seeing these tools clearly. It's one thing to believe we're following our values or reading our maps accurately—it's another to know where our navigation is actually taking us in terms of how others view our leadership. This is where the Leadership Circle Profile becomes invaluable.

The assessment begins with 120 questions, rated on a five-point scale. You start by completing a self-assessment. Then, ten to twelve carefully selected colleagues—including your boss, peers, and direct reports—provide anonymous feedback using the same questions. From this comprehensive feedback, the Leadership Circle Profile generates a powerful circular graph that maps your leadership landscape.

In this visual representation, the top half of the circle—representing the creative mind—is divided into five key dimensions:

- **Relating:** Connecting authentically with others

- **Self-awareness:** Leading with purpose and vision

- **Authenticity:** Anchoring in personal truth

- **Systems awareness:** Focusing on the whole

- **Achieving:** Bringing desired results into reality

These dimensions reflect leadership capabilities that drive effectiveness and growth.

The bottom half of the circle—representing the reactive mind—reveals the internal operating system that can limit our leadership impact. It's organized into three primary dimensions: complying (gaining worth through others' approval), protecting (maintaining distance and staying safe), and controlling (driving hard for results at all costs). These reactive tendencies, each expressed through specific protective behaviors, often emerge from experiences in our early lives. They can unconsciously drive our leadership actions, even when they no longer serve us or our organizations.

Because it includes the insights of others in your professional circle, the Leadership Circle Profile not only provides an overview of your leadership tendencies but also reveals any gaps between how you see yourself and how others experience your leadership. This can provide invaluable insights for growth and development. This fundamental truth—that our leadership development depends on the perspectives and engagement of others—points to a critical element of growth. While tools such as the Leadership Circle Profile harness collective wisdom through structured feedback, the journey of refining our mental maps and calibrating our compass requires an even deeper form of collaborative learning. This is where the power of a peer group becomes invaluable.

WHAT WORKS

- Strong People Skills
- Visionary
- Team Builder
- Personable/Approachable
- Leads by Example
- Passion
- Good Listener

- Develops People
- Empowers People
- Positive Attitude
- Motivator
- Calm Presence
- Person of Integrity
- Servant Leader

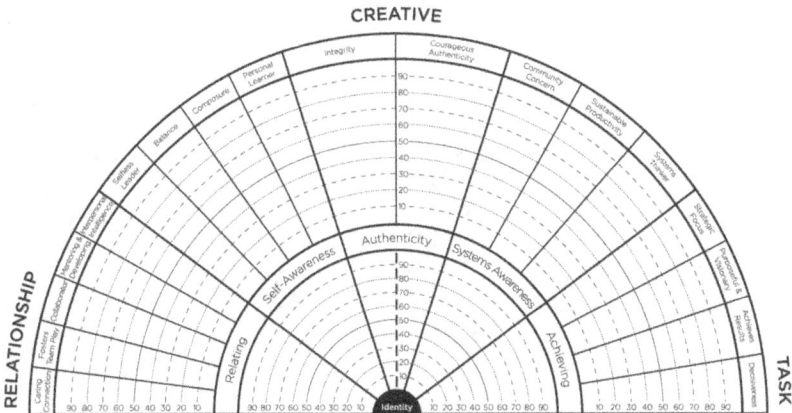

Low Balance | 10 20 30 40 50 60 70 80 90 | High Balance

Relationship-Task Balance

Creative

Reactive-Creative Scale

10 20 30 40 50 60 70 80 90

Reactive

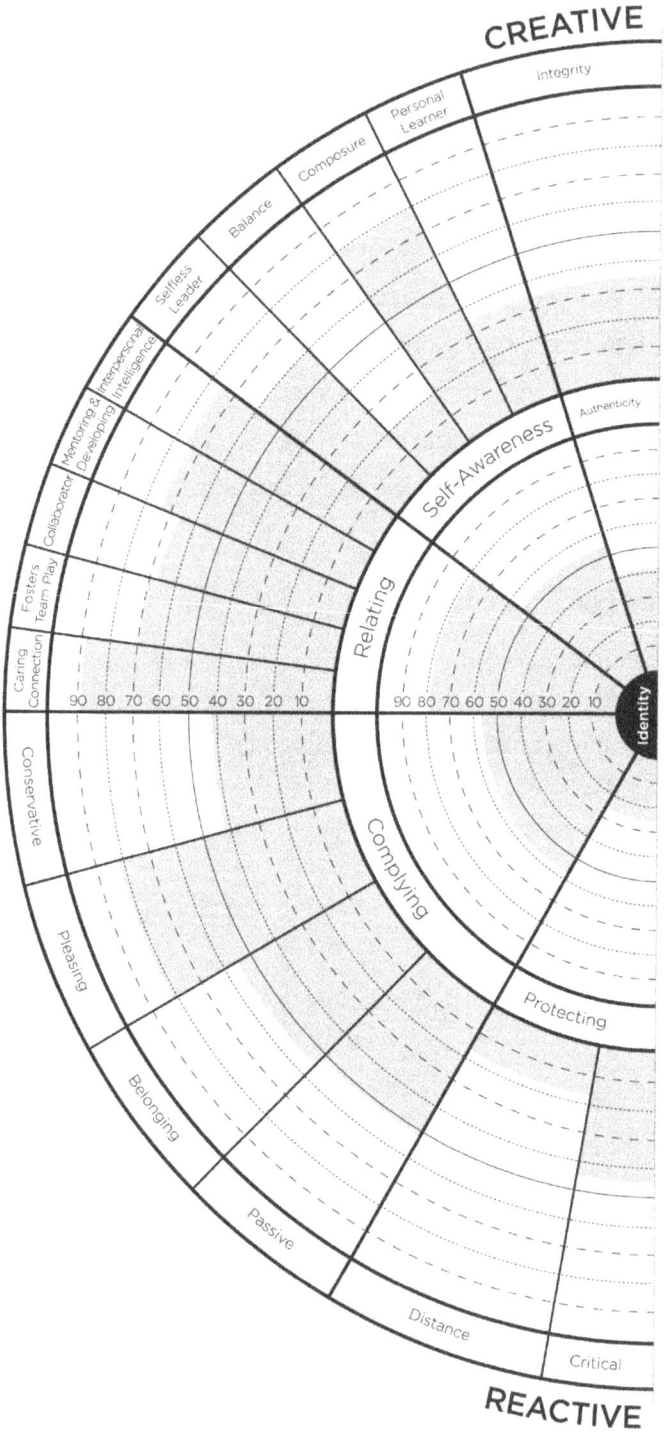

CREATIVE

Integrity

Personal Learner

Composure

Balance

Selfless Leader

Mentoring & Developing

Interpersonal Intelligence

Collaborator

Fosters Team Play

Caring Connection

90 80 70 60 50 40 30 20 10

RELATIONSHIP

Conservative

Pleasing

Belonging

Passive

Distance

Critical

REACTIVE

Self-Awareness

Authenticity

Relating

90 80 70 60 50 40 30 20 10

Identity

Complying

Protecting

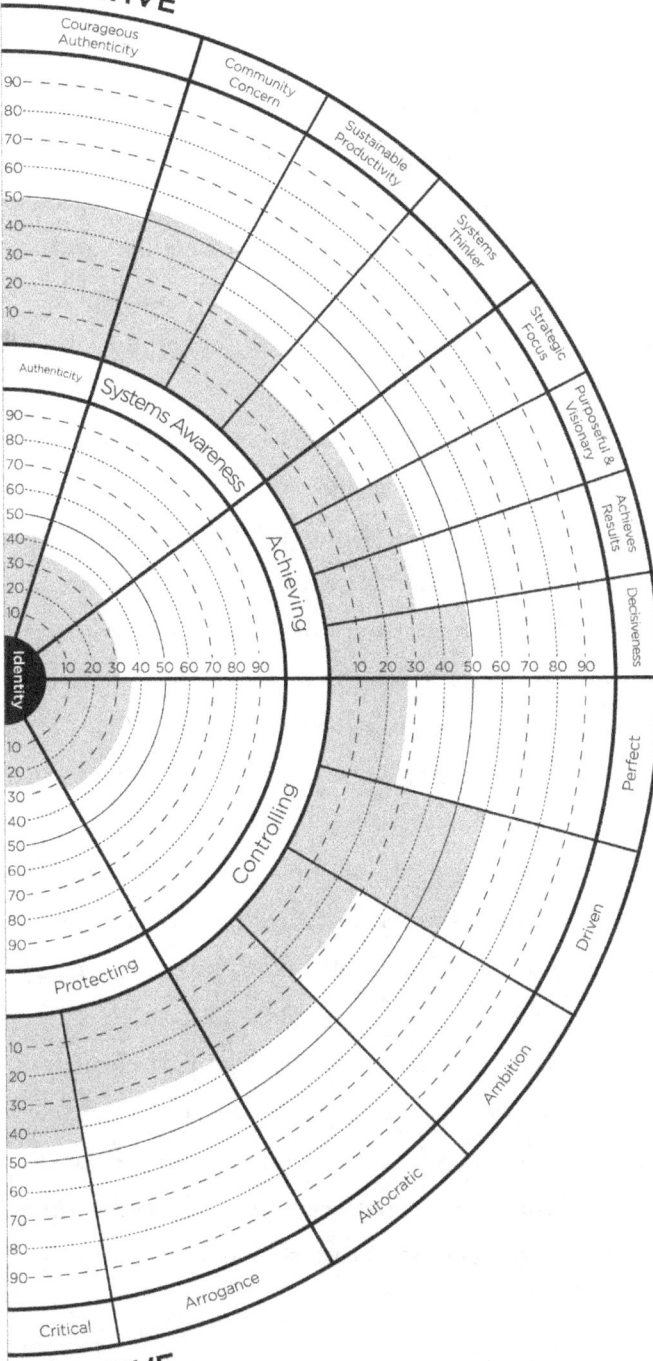

CREATIVE

Courageous Authenticity
Community Concern
Sustainable Productivity
Systems Thinker
Strategic Focus
Purposeful & Visionary
Achieves Results
Decisiveness

Authenticity
Systems Awareness
Achieving
Identity
Controlling
Protecting

Perfect
Driven
Ambition
Autocratic
Arrogance
Critical

TASK

REACTIVE

Leadership Potential Utilization

Low · 10 · 20 · 30 · 40 · 50 · 60 · 70 · 80 · 90 · High

Leadership Effectiveness

Low · 10 · 20 · 30 · 40 · 50 · 60 · 70 · 80 · 90 · High

THE POWER OF PEERS

I like to think of a peer group as a crucible—a holding space where transformation happens. Just as ancient alchemists used crucibles to transform base metals into gold, a well-facilitated peer group, such as Vistage, creates the conditions for profound personal and leadership growth. The Vistage Chair serves as a kind of alchemist, and the group becomes a safe container where we can explore the unknown territories of our leadership, bringing our fears, uncertainties, and challenges into the light.

What makes this container so powerful is its unique combination of support and challenge. Fellow leaders hold space for our vulnerability while insisting—respectfully and with dignity—that we continue to grow. When we feel held in this way, we're more willing to examine our mental maps, question our assumptions, and test our internal compass. We're more likely to voice the fears that have remained hidden and explore the territories we've been avoiding.

This shared journey accelerates our development in ways that solitary reflection cannot. When we bring our challenges to the group, we don't just receive advice—we gain multiple perspectives that help us expand our maps and refine our sense of direction. We realize we're not alone in our struggles, and this understanding gives us the courage to act on our insights.

Whether working with an executive coach or participating in a peer group (or, ideally, both), having guides and fellow travelers on this journey is invaluable. While tools, such as the Leadership Circle Profile, can illuminate our path, it's the sustained support and challenge from coaches and peers that help us actually navigate the territory.

Mastery of the inner game trumps mastery of the outer game with respect to leadership development. This kind of thing cannot be trained; it must be developed over time. My twenty years as a CEO coach and Vistage Chair have proven to me that no leader should ever walk alone. A qualified guide and a group of committed peers trying to accomplish the same thing will make the journey so much more doable and enjoyable.

INNER GAME, OUTER IMPACT

Our inner game patterns often manifest directly in our outer game behaviors. Let me share two examples from my own leadership journey that illuminate this connection. Early in my career, my self-talk insisted that asking for help showed weakness or neediness. While learning to enlist support and build collaborative relationships required developing specific outer game skills, the real shift had to happen first in my inner game—challenging and redefining my beliefs about strength and independence.

Similarly, when I needed to master the skill of delivering performance reviews, the technical aspects—the step-by-step process of giving feedback—were actually the easier part. The bigger challenge lay in my inner game: overcoming my aversion to potentially hurting someone's feelings. Until I addressed this internal barrier, no amount of outer game skill development could make me an effective communicator of difficult truths.

This inner compass, refined through experience and conscious development, doesn't just guide us through familiar terrain—it helps us navigate the uncertainties and challenges that lie ahead. And as we'll see when we explore the outer game, this internal clarity becomes the foundation for all effective leadership action.

THE OUTER GAME: ESSENTIAL SKILLS FOR THE JOURNEY

We just explored how our inner game provides both the compass of values and mental maps that guide us. But knowing where we want to go is different from knowing how to get there. The outer game is about the practical skills and competencies required to navigate the terrain effectively. On the Camino, this meant knowing how to pace myself, manage blisters, and maintain stamina for the long journey. In leadership, it means mastering fundamental capabilities that enable us to turn vision into reality.

I built much of my understanding of these practical skills during my thirty-year journey in the telecom industry, where I was tasked with taking early-stage concepts and guiding them to maturity. This experience revealed three fundamental competencies that form the foundation of effective leadership execution.

1. **Vision and Strategy**

   Creating a shared vision isn't just about having good ideas—it's about knowing how to bring together the key creative competencies identified in the Leadership Circle Profile: relating authentically with stakeholders, maintaining self-awareness about our own biases and assumptions, showing up with authenticity that builds trust, understanding systems and how different parts interconnect, and achieving results through effective execution.

   In telecom, this meant learning how to translate technical concepts into compelling business opportunities, how to engage stakeholders in developing the vision, and how to create practical road maps that turned possibilities into realities. These practical applications demonstrate how the creative dimensions work together to transform abstract possibilities into concrete achievements.

2. Communication Skills

Effective leadership requires knowing how to create the conditions for real communication. This means mastering specific skills: how to ask questions that deepen understanding, how to listen in ways that make others feel truly heard, and how to adapt your communication style to different audiences. When presenting new telecom concepts, success came not from presenting perfect plans but from knowing how to engage others in meaningful dialogue that shaped better outcomes.

3. Decision-Making

The art of decision-making is about knowing how to blend analysis with intuition effectively. In telecom's rapidly evolving landscape, I learned specific approaches: how to gather and analyze relevant data, how to weigh competing priorities, how to assess risks, and, crucially, how to move forward decisively even with incomplete information. This meant developing practical frameworks for when to rely on data versus experience and how to balance speed with thoroughness in different situations.

These aren't just theoretical concepts—they're practical skills that can be learned, practiced, and refined over time. Like learning how to properly adjust your backpack or maintain a sustainable pace on the Camino, these capabilities determine how effectively you can move forward on your leadership journey. While our inner game gives us direction and purpose, these outer game skills enable us to actually make progress along the path.

THE ALL-WEATHER GEAR: ADAPTABILITY AND RESILIENCE

Just as my Camino packing list included gear for every weather condition, effective leadership requires two essential qualities that help us navigate any circumstance: adaptability and resilience. Like the right socks and rain gear, these attributes protect us and keep us moving forward regardless of the terrain ahead. Just as I had to adapt my Camino strategy when conditions shifted—sometimes multiple times in a single day—effective leaders must be able to pivot and respond quickly to changing circumstances.

I witnessed this kind of adaptability in action while coaching a Vistage member who faced a major organizational transformation. When his company was acquired, he had to rapidly shift his leadership approach—shedding outdated beliefs, embracing new strategic priorities, and empowering his team to execute an ambitious integration plan. His ability to adapt, coupled with his unwavering commitment to the company's purpose, enabled him to steer his organization through turbulent waters and emerge even stronger.

Yet, adaptability alone isn't enough. Just as I had to endure blisters and fatigue on the Camino, leaders must also cultivate the resilience to persist through challenges. Another leader I worked with exemplified this journey of developing both qualities. Initially, he relied solely on his intellectual prowess, crowding out others' opinions with his critical, protective stance. Over time, he learned to adapt his approach, becoming more curious about others' perspectives. His resilience showed in his willingness to push through the discomfort of changing deeply ingrained habits. By the time our work together concluded, he had transformed into one of the most collaborative leaders I've known.

Like using a proper walking technique on the Camino, neither adaptability nor resilience is something we're born with—they're capacities we develop through practice. My third Camino revelation centered on finding joy in the daily walking, and the same principle applies to leadership: You have to put in the miles. You can't just read about these qualities in a book or learn them in a seminar. They must be developed through your actual day-to-day experience, through facing challenges and learning from them.

This kind of resilience isn't about being invincible. Rather, it's about developing the capacity to bounce back from setbacks, learn from failures, and maintain determination even when facing daunting circumstances. It requires the courage to try new approaches, the humility to course correct when needed, and the discipline to stay focused on a long-term vision while managing short-term challenges.

Together, adaptability and resilience form the all-weather gear of leadership—essential protection that enables us to navigate any terrain we encounter on our leadership journey. Like the right socks preventing blisters and the right jacket keeping us dry, these qualities don't just help us survive challenges—they enable us to find joy and purpose in the journey itself.

THE INTANGIBLES: THREE INTRINSIC VALUES OF LEADERSHIP

Beyond the practical tools, such as a compass, map, and gear, lie three intrinsic values I discovered while preparing to colead the Vistage Stanford Executive Leadership Program for select Vistage members in the Mid-Atlantic region. We explored a tool that helped me distill the essence of this inner/outer dynamic, drawing inspiration from Hemingway's famous six-word stories. We were challenged to capture our leadership experiences in just a half-dozen words, and when I engaged with this exercise, the story that crystallized for me was "Curious Mind, Instinctual Gut, Open Heart."

THREE INTRINSIC VALUES OF LEADERSHIP

1. Curious Mind

2. Instinctual Gut

3. Open Heart

These three wisdom centers represent my core intrinsic values of leadership. The Curious Mind embodies our endless capacity for learning and growth. The Instinctual Gut reflects our deeper wisdom and discernment, honed through experience. And the Open Heart speaks to our authentic presence and empathy in relationships. These values have proven instrumental in helping the leaders I work with navigate both the technical and human aspects of their roles. Together, they form a crucial foundation for the complete leadership presence required in today's complex, rapidly evolving business environment.

I think these values are essential to any successful leader—but this wasn't always my leadership stance. My journey through these three wisdom centers reflects the kind of transformational work that distinguishes true leadership development from mere training.

My Curious Mind was my first wisdom center, although I'm not sure how curious it was at first. I initially relied heavily on intellectual horsepower—being the smart guy in the room was my default approach. *You're going to do it because I'm the smartest person here* was my unspoken mantra, coupled with *I know how to get things done, so let's get on with it.*

While this approach drove results, it came at a considerable cost to both me and my teams. I would later learn that even the sharpest intellect becomes more powerful when tempered with curiosity.

The Instinctual Gut emerged as my second wisdom center. As Susan Scott notes in *Fierce Conversations*, you don't trust your instincts, you obey your instincts.[10] Trusting implies a passive acceptance—hearing something and assuming it must be true. Obeying, on the other hand, means actively choosing to act on that inner guidance in the moment. This profound shift from merely having intuition to actually listening to and abiding by it transformed my leadership.

These moments, when I have a kind of awareness or thought bubble that I've learned to pay attention to, are like intuitive hits. They aren't necessarily answers or specific directions; rather, they're signals to get curious and explore deeper. For instance, if I'm in a conversation with a CEO and something they say triggers that inner alertness, I don't jump to conclusions. Instead, I lean in with curiosity, asking them to elaborate. This approach has proven invaluable, such as when I asked my Chinese American client to tell me their view of authority—a question that opened up crucial insights.

This capacity to leverage intuition is a hallmark of what Jim Collins, in *Good to Great*, identifies as Level 5 leaders.[11] The most creative and effective leaders have developed this ability to recognize and act on these intuitive signals, not as definitive answers but as invitations to deeper exploration.

The Open Heart was my final and perhaps most powerful development. This wasn't about being soft—it was about having the courage to be seen, to let others see and know what truly matters to me. I discovered that vulnerability, far from being a weakness, was actually a leadership superpower. When I began letting people see my passion and being honest about how their performance or behaviors impacted

---

10   Susan Scott, *Fierce Conversations: Achieving Success at Work & in Life, One Conversation at a Time* (Berkley Books, 2004), 77.

11   Collins, *Good to Great: Why Some Companies Make the Leap ... and Others Don't.*

me and the organization when I felt let down, something remarkable happened: People became more open to me, not less. This accessibility, this capacity for genuine connection, transformed my leadership effectiveness in ways that intellectual prowess alone never could.

This evolution—from leading with intellect alone to embracing intuition to opening my heart—represents the profound identity shifts that true development requires. These identities are challenging to let go of, particularly when they've brought us success. But that's precisely what distinguishes true leadership development from training: the willingness to evolve beyond our comfortable, proven strategies to embrace more expansive ways of leading.

These three values work in concert, each strengthening the others. A curious mind helps us question our gut reactions and expand our capacity for empathy. Our instincts become sharper through both intellectual exploration and emotional awareness. And an open heart makes us more receptive to new learning while helping us apply our experience with wisdom and care. Together, these qualities enable us to navigate the complex terrain of leadership with greater skill and purpose.

Just as I learned to scrutinize every item in my Camino backpack—weighing its necessity against its burden—effective leadership often requires us to examine what we're carrying and why. The journey demands that we distinguish between essential and nonessential leadership tools. Sometimes, our greatest growth comes not from acquiring new capabilities but from leaving behind the outdated beliefs, impoverished definitions, and reactive tendencies that no longer serve us. There's profound power in this simplicity.

Like the Camino itself, which strips away life's complexities until only the essential remains—walking, connecting, reflecting—leadership becomes clearest when we focus on what truly matters: our purpose, our impact, and our relationship with those we serve. As you prepare for your own leadership journey ahead, remember that the goal isn't to accumulate every possible tool but to master the essential ones that will serve you best. Pack your leadership backpack with intention, knowing that what you choose not to carry is just as important as what you bring.

REFLECTION QUESTIONS/EXERCISES

1. Assess your current leadership tool kit. What are the key elements of your inner compass and map?

2. Identify areas for development in both your inner and outer games. Where do you need to build new skills or expand your mindsets?

3. Create a personalized Leadership Pilgrimage Map—a plan for your ongoing growth and development as a leader.

In our next chapter, we'll take a deeper dive into working with our map and compass when we focus on the inner (and outer) game of leadership.

CHAPTER 2

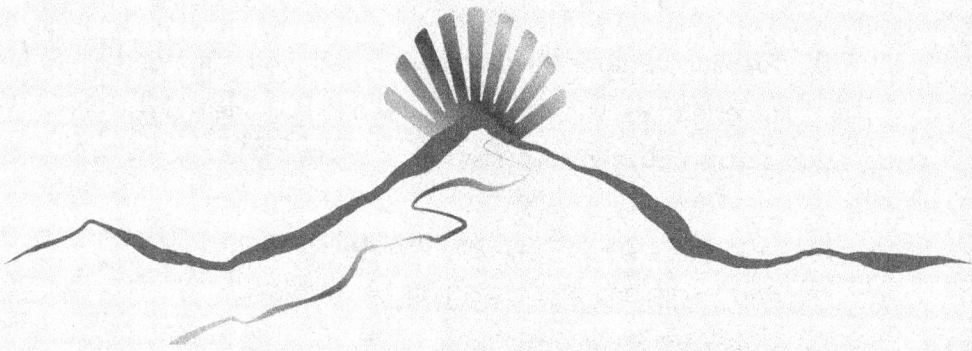

THE INNER AND OUTER GAMES OF LEADERSHIP

> *The past is not a burden; it is a scaffold which brought us to this day. We are free to be who we are—to create our own life out of our past and out of the present.*

—DAVID WHYTE

As I mentioned in the last chapter, the Camino provided countless lessons about leadership, particularly about the interplay between our inner and outer games. One of the most profound lessons came about a week into my journey.

Like many first-time pilgrims, I had arrived in Spain armed with detailed guidebooks that prescribed specific daily distances and suggested stopping points that would ensure I reached my destination on schedule. Being someone who traditionally followed the rules, I initially approached each day with a fixed mindset: I would walk exactly as far as the guidebook suggested, no more, no less. This was my outer game—the visible behaviors and actions I thought would lead to success. It was also based on an inner game belief that promised I'd achieve my desired goal so long as I followed the rules.

For six or seven days, I stuck with the program like a drill sergeant following protocol. I walked exactly as far as the guidebook said, no more, no less. Even if I felt like stopping in a charming town, or turning in early because my knees hurt, or continuing past a predetermined destination because I wanted to see more, I resisted those urges.

Then I had a revelation:

> This wasn't the guidebook's Camino—
> it was my Camino; it was mine to walk.

From that moment on, I approached my day's walking more intuitively. Some days, I felt like going a little further, and others, not as far. There was always a place to stay, whether it was a pilgrim hotel or, occasionally, a less comfortable (but character-building) night in a hostel. And I still reached my destination on schedule.

This shift from external guidance to internal wisdom mirrored a fundamental truth about leadership: While technical skills and external benchmarks matter, true leadership development requires us to examine and often transform our inner mental models—such as when I confronted my rigid concept of the right way to walk the Camino.

This interplay between inner and outer games lies at the heart of effective leadership. As I explained in the last chapter, the outer game involves visible skills and behaviors—the technical aspects of leading. But it's our inner game—our mental models, beliefs, and the stories we tell ourselves—that often determines how effectively we can deploy those skills in the real world.

INSIDE OUR INTERNAL OPERATING SYSTEM

I've already introduced the idea of the internal operating system of performance, the mental models we formed during childhood to keep us safe, secure, and worthwhile. While I touched on this concept briefly in the last chapter, it deserves deeper exploration because these mental maps and rule books often determine whether we reach our intended destination or find ourselves lost along the way.

The leaders I work with often operate from mental models about what leadership should look like that resemble my initial approach to the Camino—they're fixed and static and, therefore, limiting. These models are formed through experience, shaped by our successes and failures as they shape and reinforce our idea of what works. And because they do work for so long, they become so ingrained that we forget they're models at all. We see them as the way things are.

I've observed that leaders' mental models often manifest in what Bob Anderson calls the "reactive operating system," represented by the half circle at the bottom half of the 360-degree Leadership Circle Profile we explored in the last chapter. This reactive system consists of three primary components: the need to be liked, the need to be right, and the need for control. Let's break down what these might look like.

1. **The Need to Be Liked**

   This shows up as an overemphasis on maintaining harmony at the expense of necessary conflict or difficult conversations. One CEO I worked with struggled for months to address an underperforming executive because his mental model equated being liked with being a good leader. Only when he expanded his definition of leadership to include serving the greater good of the organization could he take necessary action.

2. **The Need to Be Right**

   This shows up as the compulsion to always be the smartest person in the room—an affliction I personally struggled with early in my career, as I mentioned. Leaders with this mental model often stifle innovation and discourage diverse perspectives by limiting the ideas they'll ever consider entertaining to their own. This inadvertently creates the very problems these leaders are trying to solve.

3. **The Need for Control**

This appears as micromanagement and an inability to delegate effectively. Like my initial approach to the Camino, when I tried to control every aspect of the journey according to the guidebook, leaders with this mental model often create bottlenecks and burn themselves out.

It's important to understand that reactive tendencies aren't character flaws—they're often the very qualities that helped us succeed early in our careers. As Collins noted in *Good to Great*, these traits can get you promoted, but they won't serve you well once you're in a leadership role.[12] The key is recognizing that these mental models need to evolve. Just as I had to evolve my mental model of how to walk the Camino—from rigidly following external guidelines to trusting my inner wisdom—leaders must evolve their reactive tendencies into more mature leadership capabilities. And, as I mentioned in this chapter, this evolution is about expansion as opposed to replacement.

4. **The Need to Be Liked Expands into Authentic Relationship Building**

When we expand our model of relationships beyond seeking approval, we can build deeper, more authentic connections with people. Instead of avoiding difficult conversations to maintain harmony, we learn to see constructive conflict and honest feedback as expressions of genuine care for others' growth.

---

12   Collins, *Good to Great: Why Some Companies Make the Leap … and Others Don't.*

5. **The Need to Be Right Expands into Collaborative Achievement**

   The evolution from needing to be the smartest person in the room to facilitating collective wisdom represents a profound shift in mental models. Instead of viewing leadership as having all the answers, we begin to see it as creating the conditions for others to contribute their best thinking. This shift allows us to achieve results through others rather than despite them.

6. **The Need for Control Expands into Developing Others**

   Perhaps the most challenging evolution is from controlling outcomes to enabling others' growth. This requires us to expand our mental model of responsibility—going from carrying all the weight ourselves to creating conditions where others can step up and learn from both successes and failures. As on the Camino, we learn that there isn't just one right way to reach our destination.

THE CONNECTION BETWEEN THE INNER AND OUTER GAMES

While these mental models live in our inner game, they directly impact our outer game behaviors. A leader who fears being disliked might avoid giving necessary feedback, while one trapped in the need to be right might shut down valuable input from their team. The outer game skills—such as how to deliver feedback or run effective meetings—don't really matter if our inner game isn't aligned with their purpose.

This is why true leadership development must address both dimensions. We need the technical skills of the outer game, but we also need to examine and evolve the mental models that determine how effectively we can deploy those skills. Like my Camino revelation about following my own path rather than the guidebook's prescriptions, the journey of leadership requires us to examine and often transcend our initial mental maps.

The goal is not to eliminate our reactive tendencies—they're part of being human—but to expand them into more mature capabilities that serve both ourselves and those we lead. For example, remember the impoverished definitions I talked about in the last chapter—limited understandings of key leadership concepts that constrain our effectiveness? A difficult childhood left me with an impoverished view that the word *responsibility* was an unwelcome burden; something to avoid as much as possible in my adult life.

Then I saw how Stephen Covey broke the word down into two words: *response* and *ability*, which gave responsibility a whole new meaning—the ability to choose how we respond to situations. This reframing helped me expand my own impoverished definition of responsibility from a burden to carry to the capacity to respond.

Each one of us has our own impoverished definitions of authority, power, or success that limit our effectiveness. The key to growth lies in recognizing and expanding these definitions, and to do that, a leader needs self-awareness.

THE POWER OF SELF-AWARENESS

Just as walking the Camino required constant attention to my body's signals—knowing when to push forward and when to rest—effective leadership demands a heightened awareness of our internal state and its impact on others. We touched on emotional regulation in chapter 1; now let's explore how this actually works in practice through a concrete example of my own journey with anger.

In my early days as a leader, I could be easily triggered. When results weren't meeting expectations, I would come across as harsh and punitive. Like many leaders, I had the technical skills to analyze performance issues, but my delivery—my outer game—was undermining my effectiveness because my inner game wasn't aligned.

The transformation began with a crucial realization: Anger itself wasn't the problem; it was simply information in the leadership context. The key was learning to relate to it differently.

This started with making an essential distinction: I wasn't angry at the people; I was angry at the results. This might seem like a subtle shift, but it transformed both how I experienced anger and how I expressed it. Instead of suppressing the emotion, I learned to channel it constructively. "How could you deliver these pathetic results?" became "I'm frustrated about these results, and we need to talk about them."

When people understood that my passion was directed at the outcome rather than at them personally, they felt safe enough to engage in productive problem-solving rather than defaulting to self-defense.

One of the most powerful lessons I learned was the importance of being transparent about this growth process. I openly acknowledged to my team, "I realize that when I get angry, you naturally want to defend yourself. That's not my intention. If I seem angry, it's because I care deeply about our results." This transparency served multiple purposes:

- It helped others understand and contextualize my emotional expressions.

- It demonstrated that leadership development is an ongoing journey.

- It created psychological safety by acknowledging and addressing people's fears directly.

Many leaders operate on autopilot, moving from meeting to meeting with a one-size-fits-all approach to the never-ending list of things they have to do. Like a pilgrim mindlessly following guidebook instructions without considering terrain or weather conditions, this automatic behavior limits our effectiveness. True self-awareness requires us to slow down and be intentional about each context we're about to enter. This means taking even just five or ten seconds before important interactions to ask ourselves these questions:

- What outcome am I trying to create here?

- What version of myself needs to show up?

- What emotional triggers might I encounter?

- How can I channel my passion productively?

These are all examples of the deployment of self into circumstance I mentioned in chapter 1. They represent a crucial shift from reactive to creative leadership. Instead of being driven by our automatic reactions, we learn to create the outcomes that matter most.

DEVELOPING SELF-AWARENESS AS AN INNER GAME TOOL

Like any tool, self-awareness requires intentional practice to master. This practice happens at three levels.

1. **Preparation**

   Before entering any significant leadership context, we practice intentional self-deployment. This means pausing to consider what version of ourselves needs to show up. It's like checking your equipment (and your feet) before each day's walk—a brief but crucial assessment that can prevent problems down the trail.

2. **In-the-Moment Awareness**

This is the ability to watch yourself be yourself in real time—observing your reactions, emotions, and impact without judgment. Think of it as maintaining awareness of your walking posture and pace while navigating difficult terrain. Are you tensing up unnecessarily? Are you moving too fast for the conditions?

3. **Course Correction**

The ultimate goal isn't perfect performance—it's the simple ability to adjust when we notice we're off track. Just as I learned to adjust my pace or take breaks when I needed to on the Camino, effective leaders learn to modify their approach when they notice their current deployment isn't creating the desired outcomes.

These inner game tools are powerful. However, as I mentioned in the last chapter, they're extremely difficult to develop on your own. We all have blind spots that are, by definition, invisible to us. We need mirrors—trusted others who can reflect back what they observe about our impact and effectiveness. These partners in development help us by

- identifying patterns we might miss,

- challenging our limiting assumptions,

- providing support as we practice new approaches, and

- celebrating progress and encouraging continued growth.

They can help us expand beyond the boundaries of our internal operating system, often by accessing the three wisdom centers I discovered through my six-word story, "Curious Mind, Instinctual Gut, Open Heart."

THE THREE WISDOM CENTERS: TOOLS FOR MOVING FROM REACTIVE TO CREATIVE

Our reactive tendencies are there to keep us safe. At the same time, they're the very things that hold us back from accomplishing everything we want. We all want to do great things but from a safe place. The push-pull between our reactive tendencies and our desire to do great things is the creative tension we all face between safety and purpose, which exists in every human being.

It's also where our three wisdom centers—Curious Mind, Instinctual Gut, and Open Heart—become vital tools for transformation, moving beyond purely rational, cognitive, Western approaches to embrace the Eastern idea of multiple forms of intelligence. Let's explore them one at a time.

1. **The Curious Mind: Beyond the Need to Know**

   A truly curious mind recognizes that it doesn't know everything—that the frame we're currently holding may not be the one needed for the context we're facing. The contrast between reactive and creative curiosity reveals itself in how leaders approach challenges. Consider these contrasting questions:

   The *reactive mind* asks, *How do I best make this decision?*

   The *creative mind* asks, *How does the best decision get made?*

   While both questions appear to seek guidance, the reactive version centers on "I"—protecting our need to be seen as likable, smart, or accomplished. The creative version opens up possibilities beyond our own capabilities. This subtle shift represents a profound movement from seeking answers that reinforce our beliefs to asking questions that genuinely explore new territory.

2. **The Instinctual Gut: From Hearing to Obeying**

The Instinctual Gut is perhaps our most frequently ignored wisdom center. It's not that we don't have instincts—we all do. The challenge lies in our willingness to obey them rather than merely hear them. In reactive leadership, our instincts often get drowned out by the louder voices of our protective identities: our need to be likable, smart, or accomplished.

I experienced this tension vividly on the Meseta—the vast plains of northern Spain. One morning, I faced a daunting twenty-mile stretch with no towns in between, longer than any distance I'd walked before. My body was tired. The heat was intense. Fear whispered in my ear, *Stay put*. But my instinct said clearly, *Go, it will be fine*. Following that instinct led to one of my most profound Camino moments.

The Meseta in late August is like walking through Kansas—flat, brown wheat fields stretching to the horizon, not a cloud in the ninety-degree sky. As I walked, occasional winds would sweep across from the left, offering blessed moments of cooling relief. Around the third or fourth time this wind came, it sparked my memory of a poem by Antonio Machado called "The Wind, One Brilliant Day."[13]

The Wind, One Brilliant Day
—Antonio Machado

The wind, one brilliant day, called
to my soul with an odor of jasmine.
"In return for the odor of my jasmine,
I'd like all the odor of your roses."
"I have no roses; all the flowers
in my garden are dead."

---

13   Antonio Machado, "The Wind, One Brilliant Day," in *Times Alone: Selected Poems of Antonio Machado*, trans. Robert Bly (Wesleyan University Press, 1983), 85.

"Well then, I'll take the withered petals
and the yellow leaves and the waters of the fountain."
The wind left. And I wept. And I said to myself:
"What have you done with the garden that was entrusted to you?"

This happened during what I call the *spiritual phase* of my Camino. For two or three days on the Meseta, I had been taking inventory of my life—the good and the bad. The rhythmic walking had put me in a meditative state in which hours would pass without my noticing. When the wind came again after that poem surfaced, I faced it and shouted at the top of my lungs:

"This is what I'm doing with the garden that was entrusted to me!"

It was a moment of profound clarity and purpose—one that would never have happened had I listened to my fear instead of my instinct that morning.

When working with leaders struggling with decisions, I often ask them, "What's your instinct?" Because I've learned that they usually know what needs to be done. I remind them of what Susan Scott says: *you don't trust your instincts, you obey them.* The key isn't achieving perfection—it's making forward progress by acting on that deeper knowing.

THE OPEN HEART: EMBRACING COURAGE AND TRUTH

The Open Heart is about courage—which is derived from the French word *coeur*, meaning heart—and the willingness to engage with truth and reality despite our fears. It means risking disappointment or hurt in service of what matters most. This isn't about the absence of emotions but about experiencing them fully while creating safety for others.

Here's the thing: People want to see you unfiltered. People want to experience all of you, the truth of you. People will feel safest around you when they know exactly where you stand.

One Vistage member I worked with during the Great Recession powerfully demonstrated this principle. She was the CEO of a company that was facing serious financial uncertainty, and, initially, she tried to protect her team by hiding her fears. Through our work together, this CEO realized that by trying to shield her team from the scary reality, she was actually preventing them from fully understanding the urgency of their situation.

When the CEO finally opened her heart and shared her genuine concerns—while maintaining her belief that the team could prevail—something remarkable happened. Rather than paralyzing the team, this CEO's vulnerability created deeper engagement. The team became more invested in the outcome because they could see both the reality of the challenge and their leader's authentic commitment to them facing it together.

THE JOURNEY TO INTEGRATION

This journey from protection to openness isn't easy. Statistics suggest that only about 25 percent of leaders across all cultures and industries make this leap,[14] largely because it requires significant investment in personal development. It's essentially a spiritual tradition, demanding daily practice and commitment—much like the Camino itself.

When we access all three wisdom centers—allowing our Curious Mind to question assumptions, our Instinctual Gut to guide action, and our Open Heart to engage courageously—we expand our capacity

---

14   "The Spirit of Leadership," The Leadership Circle, July 2021, https://leadershipcircle.com/wp-content/uploads/2021/07/Spirit-of-Leadership-Whitepaper-2021-07.pdf.

for creative leadership. Moving from a reactive to a creative mind means we're no longer focused on protecting our identity but on creating what matters most to us. This shift allows unfettered access to all our wisdom centers because we're no longer filtering through the lens of self-protection.

FROM INNER TO OUTER GAME: PUTTING WISDOM INTO ACTION

While the three wisdom centers provide our internal guidance system, leadership effectiveness ultimately depends on how we translate this inner wisdom into outer action. Just as my Camino journey required both internal awareness and practical skills—such as proper pacing and blister management—leadership demands mastery of both dimensions.

Let's explore how the inner game shapes our approach to three essential outer game skills: communication, decision-making, and strategic thinking.

1. **Communication**

   One of my Camino revelations was to travel with soft eyes and to remain open to whatever I came across without any strict agenda. Effective communication begins the same way—with the ability to listen without an agenda using *soft ears*. Many leaders, particularly those who value speed and decisiveness, struggle with this. They listen through the filter of what they want to hear, seeking evidence to support their existing views rather than truly understanding what's being shared.

   I learned this lesson the hard way early in my leadership journey. When I realized I was part of the problem behind my team's results, I began forcing myself to practice genuine curiosity. I'll admit that, at first, it felt mechanical and a little unnatural. But when I discovered that better listening led to better information, which led to better decisions, it was a major breakthrough.

Here's a practical technique I share with my clients that I call "going three questions deep":

When someone asks you a question, respond with, "Say more about that." This invitation opens the door to deeper understanding.

After they answer, ask, "Why is that important to you?" This reveals their meaning-making system.

Follow up on a key word from their response with another "Why is that important?"

This practice does more than gather information—it builds relationships. When people feel genuinely heard, they feel valued, making this more than a nice-to-have skill. It's a crucial leadership capability that transforms both understanding and engagement.

2. Decision-Making

Effective leadership decisions require both analytical and intuitive capabilities. Let's break down these complementary approaches.

The analytical component deals with the technical aspects—the nuts and bolts of the situation, the facts of the case we can assemble and examine. This is our outer game tool kit: data analysis, scenario planning, risk assessment, and other concrete evaluation methods.

But there's another dimension to decision-making that goes beyond the facts. In her book *Listening to the Oracle*,[15] Diane Skafte describes it beautifully: "To receive an oracle is to receive guidance, knowledge, or illumination from a mysterious source beyond

---

15   Dianne Skafte, *Listening to the Oracle: The Ancient Art of Finding Guidance in the Signs and Symbols All Around Us* (Harper San Francisco, 1997).

the personal self." This is where our inner game—particularly the Instinctual Gut we discussed earlier—becomes crucial.

This integration of analytical and intuitive decision-making mirrors the journey from reactive to creative leadership. When operating with a reactive mindset, we might rely too heavily on analysis to protect ourselves from criticism, or we might ignore our intuition because it conflicts with our need to appear smart or accomplished. But with a creative mindset, we can access both sources of wisdom, allowing them to inform each other.

This circles back to our three wisdom centers: The Curious Mind helps us analyze data objectively, the Instinctual Gut provides that oracle guidance beyond the facts, and the Open Heart gives us courage to act on the decision once it becomes clear. The key is learning to integrate all these sources of wisdom rather than relying solely on any one of them.

Understanding the nature of decisions can transform how we make them. The word *decision* comes from the Latin *decidere*—literally meaning "to cut off." When we decide, we're cutting away all options except the one we choose. This simple insight reveals a common leadership trap: making cuts before we've fully explored what we're cutting away.

Many CEOs pride themselves on being decisive, equating speed with effectiveness. But true decisiveness isn't about how quickly we cut—it's about ensuring we've examined all viable options before making that cut. Operating from a reactive mindset, particularly the need to be seen as smart or accomplished, we might rush to demonstrate our decision-making prowess. We run the mental equations in our heads, convinced we're the smartest person in the room, and make snap judgments that leave valuable options unconsidered.

This is another place where the inner and outer games intersect. The outer game provides frameworks and analytical tools for evaluating options. But it's our inner game—our willingness to slow down, engage curiosity, and invite other perspectives—that determines how effectively we use these tools. When we're operating from a creative mindset, we're less concerned with appearing decisive and more focused on making truly effective decisions.

3. **Strategic Vision**

Just as the Camino requires both a destination and an understanding of your starting point, strategic leadership demands clarity about both where you're going and where you are. This brings us to another crucial outer game skill: creating and implementing a strategic vision.

A long-term strategic plan is fundamentally about creating a desired future. Drawing on Robert Fritz's work on structural dynamics,[16] we can understand this as a creative process with specific structural elements. A well-formed strategic vision must be

- stated in the positive,

- anchored to a timeline,

- measurable (with clear evidence procedures),

- realistic yet challenging, and

- meaningful enough to generate energy and commitment.

You start where you are, otherwise known as your current reality. Like programming a GPS, you need an accurate starting point. This requires what I call "mastering the courage to interrogate reality." Imagine your desired future floating at your forehead level, with current reality at

---

16   Robert Fritz, *Corporate Tides: The Inescapable Laws of Organizational Structure* (Berrett-Koehler, 1996).

your belly button. The distance between them creates what Fritz calls "creative tension"—a natural and necessary part of the creative process.

Understanding this tension requires a deep examination of two key elements of the current reality:

- **Supports:** What's already in place that will help you move toward the vision?

- **Inhibitors:** What obstacles must be addressed to make progress?

Let me share an example: Consider a company wanting to grow from $5 million in annual revenue to $25 million in annual revenue in five years. The supports might include marketplace position and product superiority. The inhibitors often include inadequate systems for scaling and—most crucially but often overlooked—the leadership team's own developmental needs.

This is where the inner and outer games intersect again. Many leaders do a poor job of strategic implementation because they avoid fully examining the current reality, particularly when that examination points to their own limitations. As one CEO told me, "Going from $5 million to $25 million doesn't just require upping our game—it requires upping two games: the inner game of mental models and the outer game of systems and processes."

LEADERSHIP AS A RELATIONAL SKILL

Ultimately, implementing any strategic vision depends on our ability to engage others—which brings us to perhaps the most fundamental outer game skill: relationship building. Leadership is essentially a relational skill, measured by how others experience you and your ability to inspire action toward shared goals.

The Leadership Circle Profile that we explored earlier illustrates this through its division of creative competencies: The right side represents task orientation, while the left represents relational capabilities. While we often enter adult life with a bias toward one or the other, great leadership requires capacity in both.

This mirrors Jim Collins's insights about the evolution from *good* to *great*. It's not about abandoning relationships for tasks or vice versa. Again, it's about expansion, in this case, expanding how we approach relationships.[17] *Good* might mean being likable and maintaining harmony. But *great* means building relationships based on trust and respect that can withstand difficult conversations and challenge each other to reach better outcomes.

Almost every leader comes into their role over-indexing on either relationships or tasks. I was a very task-oriented leader—good at getting stuff done, but not at valuing relationships in the way I needed to. It wasn't that I disrespected relationships; I simply didn't see them as essential to enlisting support and engaging others in the work. When you lead this way, you're not sharing. You're over controlling, not delegating, not incorporating other perspectives, and not inviting feedback. Everything depends on you and your individual results.

What I came to realize was that truly valuing relationships with my team—paying attention to them and relating to them differently—became a powerful leverage point. Improvement for every leader I've ever worked with has involved recognizing that scaling the business and expanding leadership effectiveness requires involving others. This means being open-minded to their perspectives, willing to see things differently, and committed to developing their capacity to do things even better than we can.

---

17   Collins, *Good to Great: Why Some Companies Make the Leap ... and Others Don't.*

THE ULTIMATE INTEGRATION: WHY THE INNER GAME RUNS THE OUTER GAME

As we conclude our exploration of the inner and outer games, it's crucial to understand their fundamental relationship: The inner game runs the outer game. Just as a computer's operating system determines what the computer can do, our internal operating system determines our leadership performance. While we need to master both games, the inner game often acts as a limiting factor.

This brings us to one of the most powerful concepts in leadership development: what Bob Anderson calls the "cancellation effect." This occurs when our inner game isn't developed enough to support our outer game's capabilities, effectively canceling out skills we've worked hard to acquire. Think of it like installing sophisticated software on an outdated operating system—the program might be excellent, but the operating system can't run it effectively.

Let me illustrate this with a common scenario. Consider a leader who has mastered Susan Scott's Mineral Rights approach to digging deep during fierce conversations by following a set of steps. They might know the methodology better than Scott herself—the exact steps, the precise questions, the perfect timing. That's outer game mastery. But if their inner operating system is dominated by the need to be liked, they'll never have those conversations with the impact they're designed to create. The sophisticated outer game skill gets canceled out by the limiting inner game.

The cancellation effect can show up in countless ways:

- A leader might have excellent strategic planning skills (outer game), but their need for control (inner game) prevents them from engaging others in the process.

- They might know exactly how to run effective meetings (outer game), but their need to be seen as smart (inner game) leads them to dominate discussions.

- They might be trained in delegation best practices (outer game), but their fear of losing control (inner game) results in micromanagement.

What makes the cancellation effect such a powerful concept is that it helps leaders understand their development challenges in a new way. Instead of feeling broken or inadequate, they can see that they're simply running an operating system that needs updating. This reframing often helps leaders embrace development more readily—it's not about fixing what's wrong but about upgrading their internal capacity to match their technical capabilities.

The implications are profound. Many organizations invest heavily in skill development—teaching leaders new methodologies, frameworks, and best practices—while underinvesting in the inner game development that would allow leaders to actually deploy these skills effectively. It's like continuously installing new software without upgrading the operating system.

Anderson warns, "Unless leaders are developing at a pace that matches or exceeds the complexity of their environment, they'll fail."[18] This means parallel development is required—we must continue acquiring new skills and knowledge while simultaneously updating who we are as we deploy these capabilities. The cancellation effect makes clear why this parallel development is so crucial: Without it, our sophisticated outer game tools may never achieve their intended impact.

---

18   Anderson and Adams, *Mastering Leadership: An Integrated Framework for Breakthrough Performance and Extraordinary Business Results.*

As you continue your leadership journey, remember that, like the Camino, it's not about reaching a final destination but about continuous growth and evolution. The path requires us to develop both our inner and outer games simultaneously, always expanding our capacity to meet the increasing complexity of leadership demands. Just as my Camino journey taught me to trust both my guidebook knowledge and internal wisdom, effective leadership requires us to integrate both technical skills and internal development into a coherent whole.

REFLECTION QUESTIONS/EXERCISES

1. Think of a leadership situation in which you felt your reactive tendencies (need to be liked, need to be right, or need for control) may have limited your effectiveness. How might that situation have played out differently if you had operated from your creative mindset instead? Be specific about what you would have done or said differently.

2. Consider your own cancellation effect—where might your inner game be limiting the impact of your outer game skills? For example, you may have strong delegation skills but an inner need for control prevents you from using them effectively. What would it look like to align your inner and outer games in this area?

3. Before your next significant leadership interaction, try this self-awareness practice: Take ten seconds to ask yourself, "What outcome am I trying to create here?" and "What version of myself needs to show up?" After the interaction, reflect: How did this intentional self-deployment affect the outcome? What did you notice about yourself and others?

Next, we'll begin building capacity for our leadership journey, beginning with the challenge of developing our core leadership skills.

CHAPTER 3

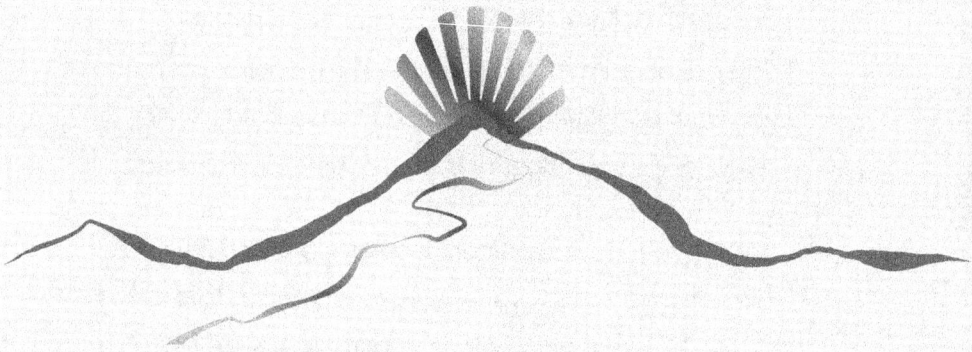

THE PHYSICAL
CHALLENGE—
DEVELOPING CORE
LEADERSHIP SKILLS

Fall seven times, get up eight.

—ZEN PROVERB

Before my trip to Spain, I had dreamed of walking the Camino for over a year. I'd done everything I could to prepare—I talked with veteran pilgrims, trained with increasingly long walks, researched the best gear, studied the guidebooks, and even practiced with my loaded backpack. The Camino had become my obsession, the adventure I wanted more than anything.

Then I got there. And I hated it.

Despite all my preparations, nothing could have readied me for how the experience of walking fifteen to twenty miles a day through rugged terrain would actually feel. The physical challenge was immense. My whole body hurt. I wasn't sleeping well at night. And as bad as I felt physically, the mental toll was worse.

I felt like I was failing the Camino.

What were you thinking? I berated myself. *You didn't prepare enough. Maybe you aren't ready to do this.* Each day just felt miserable and was filled with despondent self-talk about what an idiot I had been for thinking I could walk five hundred miles.

And yet, even in this depleted state, there were moments of pure glory. I remember walking into a village around day four or five, and they were in the middle of a festival, a running of the bulls. While I was in my head a lot, bitching and moaning, moments of wonder such as that one would still catch me and shake me out of my stupor.

Imagine how amazing it would have been if I hadn't been so damn hard on myself.

What I didn't realize was that I had fallen into a common, and very normal, trap. I thought I was failing when really all I was doing was building the capacity to do the thing. I had confused fatigue with failure.

THE PRICE OF GROWTH

Every journey has a price. To put it in poetic or spiritual language, when I signed up to walk the Camino, I contracted with the gods to go through the pain. That was the price, and I had signed up for this thing, so why was I bitching?

When I work with CEOs, I see this same pattern play out in their leadership journeys. Nearly every leader I've worked with goes through a phase where they confuse fatigue with failure. They experience the exhaustion that comes with change and growth, and they tell themselves a story that nearly talks them right out of changing. However, just as my early days on the Camino demanded physical fatigue and discomfort, leadership requires us to face the pain that comes with the rigor of developing new capabilities and confronting our limitations.

As an emerging or advancing leader, you really have two jobs. There's the work you need to do for your employer and the work you need to do on yourself. I think you have to view leadership development as a job because it requires skill-building, just like your day job. Yes, it takes time and effort, but this is the price we agree to pay when we choose the path of growth. It's our own contract with the gods.

The Four Stages of Competence: A Leadership Journey
You may have heard of the Dunning–Kruger effect—the idea that people with limited knowledge or skill in a particular area tend to overestimate their competence, while those with greater expertise are more likely to underestimate theirs. It's a helpful reminder that self-perception doesn't always line up with actual ability, especially in the early stages of learning.

DUNNING–KRUGER EFFECT

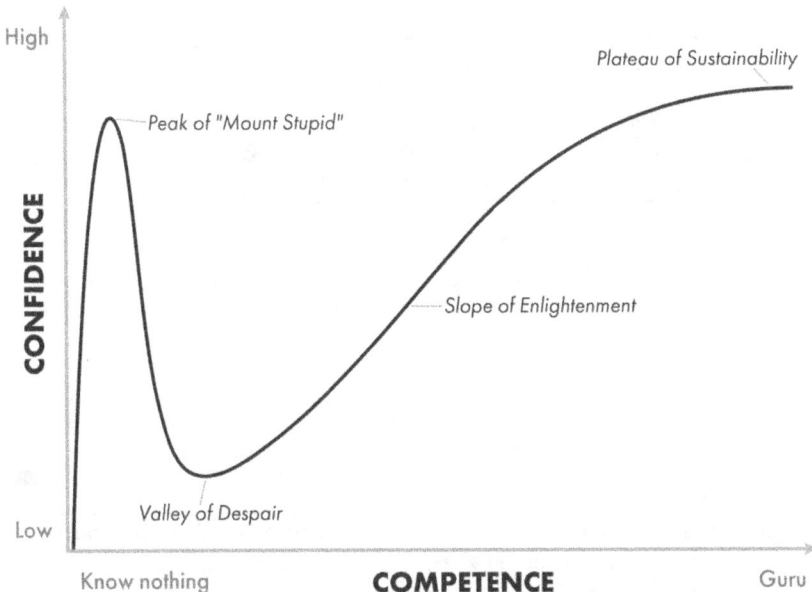

High

Plateau of Sustainability

Peak of "Mount Stupid"

CONFIDENCE

Slope of Enlightenment

Valley of Despair

Low

Know nothing   **COMPETENCE**   Guru

As you develop your leadership capability, you will experience what's known as the Four Stages of Competence model, developed by Noel Burch at Gordon Training International in the 1970s.[19] The model is based on the 1960s research of management coach Martin M. Broadwell.[20]

THE COMPETENCY LADDER

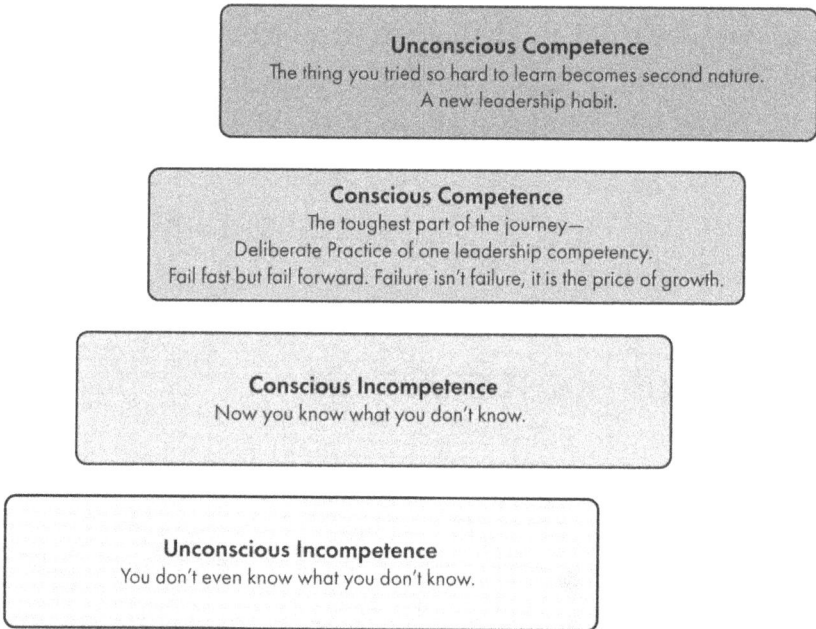

Unconscious Competence
The thing you tried so hard to learn becomes second nature.
A new leadership habit.

Conscious Competence
The toughest part of the journey—
Deliberate Practice of one leadership competency.
Fail fast but fail forward. Failure isn't failure, it is the price of growth.

Conscious Incompetence
Now you know what you don't know.

Unconscious Incompetence
You don't even know what you don't know.

---

19   Linda Adams, "Learning a New Skill is Easier Said Than Done," *Gordon Training International*, accessed April 30, 2025, https://www.gordontraining.com/free-workplace-articles/learning-a-new-skill-is-easier-said-than-done/

20   Martin Broadwell, "Teaching for Learning," *The Gospel Guardian* 20, no. 41 (1969): 1–3.

This is the way I interpret those four stages:

1. **Unconscious incompetence:** You don't even know what you don't know. This is an important thing to recognize because the moment you do is the moment that enables the journey to begin.

2. **Conscious incompetence:** You learn something through failing fast, failing forward. You now know what you don't know.

3. **Conscious competence:** Now that you know what you don't know, you can consciously build competence. This is the hardest part of the journey, intentionally paying attention to building a leadership habit. This is also where failure and fatigue come in. It's the part of the change process where most people will give up because they think they're failing when what they're really doing is learning.

4. **Unconscious competence:** Once you push through the failure and fatigue, the thing you've tried so hard to learn becomes a habit, and now you just have it.

To me, this journey to unconscious competence is the essence of what it means to become a leadership journeyman. It's this series of four-stage, competency-building challenges that never ends.

However, not all competencies are the same. Ronald Heifetz at Harvard Kennedy School identified two distinct types of challenges leaders have to address: technical challenges and adaptive challenges.[21] Now let's look at them in a little more depth.

Technical challenges are bigger, better, faster, cheaper things and only require outer game skills and knowledge. It's where the solution is known. You go out and acquire it, and you bolt it on. The solution could be training, such as how to do a spreadsheet or run a good

---

21   Ronald Heifetz, *Leadership Without Easy Answers* (Harvard University Press, 1994), 69–73.

one-to-one meeting with a direct report. There are technical skills that are required to do those things well, and you can learn how to do them because we already know that the knowledge exists out there.

Adaptive challenges are very different because, by definition, no solution exists for them. The COVID-19 pandemic was full of adaptive challenges—who thought work could be done remotely? And yet, we figured it out. Scaling is also an adaptive challenge that involves a business going from one size to the next. It's hugely complicated, and nobody's ever done it exactly the way you'll need to do it.

Adaptive challenges are where most leaders hit the wall. At an expert level, the typical response to a problem with this degree of complexity is either/or thinking—it's either this thing or that thing. During the pandemic, many people thought that either the work would get done in the office or the work wouldn't get done. The options were very limited. What's required in modern-day leadership and business is both/and thinking—the requirement to be able to hold two seemingly opposite ideas in the same space. That's how you find the solution: by incorporating what may seem like opposite ideas as part of the new way forward. Being able to embrace paradox is Level 5 stuff. It's higher-order thinking, real achiever stuff.

This process can be enabled by peer groups, where leaders regularly encounter perspectives radically different from their own. These diverse viewpoints, combined with targeted coaching, illuminate my conviction that leaders should never walk alone. Surround yourself with people who understand what it's like to be fatigued to the point of exhaustion, to not know the answer when they think they should.

That's what peer groups and executive coaches provide. When we're talking about transformational growth, whether on the Camino or in leadership, the rigor of the journey demands support. At this level, to expect to have all the answers or to be able to find all the

answers all by your lonesome is crazy and unsustainable. This reality—
that we need others to help us see our blind spots and support our
growth—leads us to what I call "the quality of innocence."

THE QUALITY OF INNOCENCE: LEARNING TO UNLEARN

One of the most powerful skills a leader can develop is the ability to let
go of every assumption about what we're supposed to be experiencing
and try to look at an issue with fresh eyes, like those of a child. On
the Camino, as I got stronger with each day's walking, I began to ask,
*How do I learn from this and continually be in that kind of practice and
discovery mode?*

This is what I mean by *soft eyes*—the absence of the need for
certainty and knowledge. Just as all those Camino guidebooks could
not really capture what the journey would actually be like for *me*, the
leadership journey is a personal one. Books and other forms of study
can prepare you, but they can't tell you what your unique experience
will be. But a lot of times, especially with CEOs, what gets in the way
is our inability to admit that we don't know. Because we're supposed
to know. We're high-paid executives; we're supposed to have an answer
for everything … aren't we?

Most leaders want clarity all the time, and that's fine, but we also
need to accept that we're not going to get it. The inability to embrace
that, to admit that we don't know, is an enemy of learning. The first
thing you need to do as a leader is recognize that there are some things
that you need to learn and that you don't know—what Jim Collins
calls "comfort with ambiguity."

Your job is not to *know* the answer; your job is to *find* the answer.
This relates to the difference between self-competence and self-efficacy.

While competence is a skill-building thing that develops over time, self-efficacy is something deeper—it's a sense of personal power in which you know you don't have the answer but have enough internal resources and world experience to believe you'll figure it out.

Almost every leader I've worked with has accomplished significant things—that's efficacy, that's their proof of personal power. But then they run into something that's really hard and forget they've done hard things before. They've been through similar things, come out the other side, and solved problems they didn't have answers to going in. And they can do it again.

COMMUNICATION: SETTING CLEAR EXPECTATIONS

Having the right mindset and inner game is essential, but leadership ultimately comes down to how effectively we communicate with others. As I said before, leadership is a relational skill. Every aspect of leadership—from setting a direction to building trust and from driving results to developing people—depends on our ability to communicate clearly and connect authentically with others.

Clear communication starts with crystal-clear expectations. I can't tell you how many times I've seen leaders frustrated with poor results, only to discover that their people weren't clear about what was expected of them in the first place. The Gallup organization found that only 50 percent of employees strongly agree that they know what's expected of them at work.[22] When people fail to deliver on expectations, most of the time it's because they simply weren't clear about what those expectations were—not because they lacked the skills or the right attitude.

---

22 "State of the American Workplace Report," Gallup, February 15, 2017, https://www.gallup.com/workplace/238085/state-american-workplace-report-2017.aspx.

There's a specific sequence I use to clarify expectations, which is an outer game skill. But setting clear expectations isn't just about stating what needs to be done. It's about helping people understand why it matters. What's the organizational impact they'll have? How will accomplishing this help grow their career? What will it feel like to know they made this contribution? That's real communication—connecting the *what* with the *why* in a way that energizes people to deliver their best work.

Another crucial communication skill is recognition, and it involves two distinct elements: a compliment and an acknowledgment. A compliment recognizes the specific task someone did at a high level. An acknowledgment speaks to something about their character that must be true for them to do that thing at that level.

For example: "Thank you for spending Friday night putting together the pricing section of this proposal. It was really accurate and well done." That's the compliment.

"What I especially appreciate is your commitment to this organization and your commitment to excellence in how we want to present ourselves as professionals." That's the acknowledgment.

It's so important to provide that kind of support, to catch your people doing things right. And we, as leaders, just don't. There isn't a CEO or a leader I've ever worked with who isn't really good at spotting what's broken and absolutely sucks at pointing out what's going right. This is an everywhere, all the time thing. We're just not wired to be oriented to look for what's going well. But we can change that. If you really want to build rapport and connection with your people, catch 'em doing something right. It might even be the thing that you've been asking them to improve on.

I was absolutely guilty of this. I was the leader who was much more focused on the task side of things—get it done; winning is everything; and forget the emotion, as I don't want to hear about any of that shit. When I started to get feedback such as "You're not connecting with your people; it would go a lot better for you if you did the people thing a little better," I realized I had to pay attention to that. And at first, it felt awkward. I actually wondered, *Am I being a little squishy here in an inappropriate way? Have I just crossed a line that I shouldn't?*

I had to essentially feel my way around until I realized that all I was doing was telling the truth about a person's character, and what could possibly be wrong with that? When that light bulb clicked on for me and I started to do it, the responses I got back made me realize, *Holy cow, why didn't I do this sooner?*

Another important communication skill is learning to care effectively without over caring. Being genuinely interested in your team's work and personal lives builds trust and connection. But over caring—becoming emotionally invested in every outcome or trying to solve everyone's problems for them—sucks your energy and undermines their growth. Effective leaders show interest and support while maintaining healthy boundaries, allowing their teams to navigate their own paths and build their own resilience, which helps them develop into better leaders themselves.

RESILIENCE IN THE NEW LEADERSHIP LANDSCAPE

Today's volatility, uncertainty, complexity, and ambiguity (VUCA) environment is marked by the sort of adaptive challenges we introduced earlier, requiring thinking completely outside the box and letting go of what worked in the past. This requires resilience.

Consider a CEO scaling their business from $5 million in annual revenue to $10 million in annual revenue. This journey inevitably involves entering situations they've never encountered before. What works at $5 million often doesn't work at $10 million—organizational structures, systems, and processes all need reinvention. Success requires a willingness to "fail fast, fail forward"[23]—as outlined in Eric Ries's *The Lean Startup*, which is essentially a process of trying something, failing, and using what you've learned to try the next thing. In other words, success comes from constantly forwarding the action while deepening the learning—and doing that, getting knocked down over and over and coming back for more, requires grit.

I recently had the opportunity to talk with academic and psychologist Angela Duckworth, whose research on grit illuminates why some leaders thrive in this environment while others falter. Her key insight? It all comes down to time. The most successful leaders display grit and resilience over extended periods. Just as on the Camino, the joy—and the growth—is in the walking. You know it's going to take time. These things don't come easy.

This resilient mindset is also captured perfectly in what Jim Collins calls the Stockdale Paradox, named after Admiral James Stockdale, who survived years as a prisoner of war. The principle? You must maintain unwavering faith that you will prevail while still confronting the brutal facts of your current reality.

I recently worked with a Vistage member whose organization faced losing half of its funding because of political changes. When discussing the future, they said, "Well, the first thing I have to do is believe I have one."

Perfect. We explored possibilities until they could see a path forward. This wasn't their first crisis—they'd survived similar cuts before, such as having to reduce their organization's workforce by half. But they

---

23 Eric Ries, *The Lean Startup: How Today's Entrepreneurs Use Continuous Innovation to Create Radically Successful Businesses* (Crown Business, 2011).

embodied the Stockdale Paradox and had absolute faith that they would prevail and prosper again while confronting brutal facts—likely contract losses, potential staff cuts of 50 percent, hard decisions ahead.

The leader's challenge is communicating both belief and reality to their team. Don't hide anything, but don't just scare people. You must fully believe in the future you're building while acknowledging current challenges. That's leadership at its core. And it demands resilience at every step.

But here's where I see many leaders stumble: Early in their journey, they're bold and adventurous, willing to make mistakes because they're driven by their goal. They play to win, and they succeed. Then something shifts. They start thinking, *I might lose this*, or *My net worth could be impacted.* They switch to playing to not lose—and that's deadly. You'll have marginal growth at best, and you're vulnerable to competitors who are still playing to win.

Playing to win means keeping that clear line of sight about why you're doing what you're doing, despite obstacles and risk. Just like my strong *why* kept me going on the Camino, successful leaders stay connected to their driving purpose. When they hit obstacles—and they will—that clarity about why they're doing this work fuels their resilience.

Here's a truth I've learned: We do not fear the unknown. What we fear is the loss of the known. I've seen this play out with countless CEOs—they become so comfortable with what they know that they think that's who they are. It becomes their identity. Even when their familiar approaches stop working, they hang on because these approaches made them special, got them where they are. They'd rather stick with what's not working than risk feeling adrift.

This mindset is completely contradictory to their self-concept of being in charge. Many leaders believe they're supposed to have all the answers—they get out of bed every day carrying these self-imposed limitations. But here's the thing: Everyone knows that's impossible, including their employees. When you stand in front of your workforce and let them know you're not entirely sure what the answer is, you haven't lost credibility. You've gained their respect. Because you haven't said, "We can't figure it out." You've said, "I don't know in the moment, but we will figure it out."

This is another example of having soft eyes, meeting the unknown with an attitude of curiosity rather than certainty. It's about asking questions and approaching challenges with genuine openness. When leaders can slow down and stop the rush of urgency or panic, they can ask themselves one essential question: *What is the main thing here?*

I use this principle constantly in my coaching. When a CEO brings me a complex situation with no obvious answer, I ask, "What's the main thing for you right now with respect to this challenge?" This helps them focus and get clear about their priority. Then comes what I consider a universal truth in leadership:

> The main thing is to keep the main thing the main thing.

Once leaders grasp this, everything else falls into place.

This clarity is powerful—I've seen it again and again in my work. Once a leader gets clear on the nature of their challenge, solutions naturally appear. They just need to get clear about what they need to pay attention to and why. This is another area where peer groups and coaches become invaluable resources. We're the ones who remember to ask these essential questions, who help leaders hear perspectives different from their own, who support them in becoming more adaptable. When leaders hit obstacles—and they will—that clarity about their main thing fuels their resilience.

MANAGING TIME THROUGH PRIORITIES

By now, you might be thinking, *This all sounds great, but who has the time?* Throughout this book, I've asked you to be more deliberate, to bring in the opinions and ideas of others, to think things through deeply. And if you're like most leaders I work with, you're already struggling to find enough hours in the day.

Here's the truth: You don't manage time; you manage priorities. We all have the same fixed number of hours, but we can radically influence how we use them. The most effective leaders I work with have internalized this fundamental shift in thinking. Instead of trying to squeeze more into each day, they get ruthlessly clear about what matters most.

The inner game challenge here is accepting that you can't do it all—and that's OK. Just as important as knowing what to do is knowing what not to do. This means taking a hard look at where you're spending your time and energy and asking yourself a crucial question: *Whose job am I doing other than my own?*

A classic *Harvard Business Review* article called "Management Time: Who's Got the Monkey?"[24] explores a perpetual puzzle in management: "Why is it that managers are typically running out of time while their subordinates are typically running out of work?" The article uses monkeys as a metaphor for employee problems and responsibilities. When employees ask you to solve their challenges, they're essentially trying to hand over their "monkey"—their problem—to you. Level 5 leaders don't take on these monkeys. Instead, they empower their workforce by saying, "That's your challenge. Let's talk about what you need to solve it, but I won't solve it for you."

---

24   William Oncken, Jr. and Donald Wass, "Management Time: Who's Got the Monkey?" *Harvard Business Review*, November–December 1974.

So, how do you protect the time you need to deliver this level of leadership? The most successful leaders I work with block their calendars strategically. They schedule their most important priorities first—whether that's strategic thinking time, key meetings with their leadership team, or focused work on critical initiatives. Everything else has to fit around these nonnegotiable blocks. They've learned that if you don't actively protect time for what's most important, the urgent matters will always crowd it out.

This intentional approach to priorities is something you have to always be watching for. That's why you have an executive coach to hold you accountable. It's why you have a peer group to keep your eyes focused on the main thing.

Here's a pattern I see all the time: CEOs spend time on the things they like to do or the things they feel competent at doing. They avoid spending time on things they don't like or don't feel they're good at. It's another universal problem, and it tracks with my Camino revelation that the joy is in the walking. You've got to be good with the everyday, ordinary parts of the job, including the stuff you don't like to do. When leaders avoid certain responsibilities, the work either doesn't get done or gets done badly. And that's when results suffer.

Even with priorities carefully calendared, there are always challenges. There's the emergency of the day, which you have to pay attention to—that's the urgent priority. But by getting clear about what only you can do, empowering your team to handle the rest, and protecting time for what matters most, you can create the space needed for both your own development and your organization's growth.

🐚

Just as my body gradually adapted to the demands of walking the Camino, leadership capability develops through consistent practice and challenge. The physical conditioning didn't happen overnight—it was built step-by-step, day by day. The same is true for the core leadership skills we've explored in this chapter. The Camino taught me that growth comes from embracing the everyday walking—including (and especially) the hard parts.

Leadership development follows the same path. It requires us to build our capacity through daily practice, welcoming the discomfort that comes with stepping outside our comfort zones and remembering that what feels like failure is often just fatigue as we develop new capabilities. Just as every pilgrim must leave behind what's familiar to walk the Camino, leaders must be willing to let go of what worked in the past to grow into what's needed now.

REFLECTION QUESTIONS/EXERCISES

1. What leadership muscles are you currently building? Where do you feel the *good pain* of growth?

2. Which of your current challenges are technical (requiring known solutions) and which are adaptive (requiring new ways of thinking)?

3. How effectively are you communicating expectations and recognition to your team?

4. How are you protecting time for your own development while managing day-to-day responsibilities?

5. What known ways of operating might you need to let go of to reach the next level?

6. Who's supporting your leadership journey? How are you leveraging peer relationships and coaching to accelerate your growth?

In our next chapter, we'll explore the powerful concept of traveling light—discovering and releasing the old patterns, beliefs, and baggage that weigh down your leadership journey.

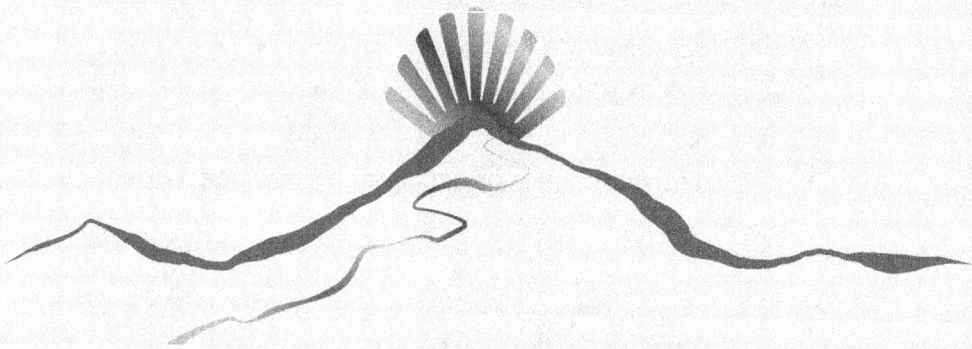

CHAPTER 4

TRAVEL LIGHT— SHEDDING UNNECESSARY BURDENS

He who would travel happily must travel light.

—ANTOINE DE SAINT-EXUPÉRY

I started this book by sharing a story from the day I climbed to Cruz de Ferro. That day, I joined my fellow pilgrims at the base of Monte Irago in the ritual of releasing a rock I had carried on my journey, symbolizing a burden I was still carrying in my life. I chose that story for a specific reason—that was the day I saw my worn-out, old face in the mirror, the defining moment of my Camino.

But the ritual of the Iron Cross is significant for another reason. It's a highlight of the journey for many pilgrims who come to the Camino for the specific purpose of releasing their burdens. They recognize that those burdens are the things that stop them from seeing clearly, from moving freely, from experiencing life as it's meant to be experienced.

The pilgrimage teaches us a fundamental truth: What you carry weighs you down—whether it's an extra pair of shoes in your backpack or pain from a difficult relationship. These unnecessary items become burdens that slow your progress and drain your energy. The same thing happens in leadership. Leaders weigh themselves down with habits of thinking, patterns of behaving, and outdated success strategies that no longer serve them. Reaching your full potential as a leader, achieving that Level 5 of leadership that Collins talks about in *Good to Great*, means finding, confronting, and ultimately ridding yourself of these burdens—because each one is standing between you and your full potential.[25]

That's why, in this chapter, we'll explore the first of my four Camino revelations: *Travel Light*. Just like that rock at the Cruz de Ferro, leaders must learn to shed the mental, emotional, and behavioral burdens that are holding them back from their true potential.

POWER VERSUS FORCE: THE ESSENTIAL DISTINCTION

Shakespeare wrote, "Uneasy lies the head that wears the crown" for good reason. Becoming a leader means gaining more power—but what exactly does *power* mean? It turns out that one of the heaviest burdens leaders carry is a fundamental misunderstanding of power. Remember the Chinese American CEO who equated power with "boots on the neck?" Like so many of the leaders I work with, that CEO had an impoverished definition of power, confusing it with *force*.

Psychiatrist David Hawkins explored this phenomenon in his book, *Power vs. Force*.[26] He presented what he called a "Map of Consciousness" that measured levels of human consciousness and awareness on a scale from one to one thousand.

---

25 Collins, *Good to Great: Why Some Companies Make the Leap ... and Others Don't*.

26 David Hawkins, *Power vs. Force: The Hidden Determinants of Human Behavior* (Hay House, 2002).

He put force below two hundred on the scale, along with traits such as shame, guilt, fear, desire, anger, and pride—below what he called the "threshold of integrity." In contrast, power (levels above two hundred) represents states, such as courage, neutrality, willingness, acceptance, reason, love, and joy, that are self-sustaining and energizing rather than depleting.[27]

This distinction is critical for leaders who want to travel light. Using force—whether through control, manipulation, or compliance-seeking—takes energy. It requires constant vigilance and reinforcement. True power flows naturally from alignment with purpose and actually creates energy rather than consuming it. When we understand this difference, we begin to see how our leadership approach might be weighing us down.

> *True power flows naturally from alignment with purpose and actually creates energy rather than consuming it.*

Hawkins's research maps directly to the Leadership Circle Profile 360-degree model we've been exploring—power is represented by the top half of the circle and force by the bottom half.

The behaviors in the bottom half are all reactive—driven by fear, insecurity, and the need for control, while the top half represents the range of creative competencies that emerge from authenticity, purpose, and vision.

Power in leadership springs from inner clarity and serves a greater purpose. It builds trust, creates a lasting impact, and channels expertise toward meaningful outcomes. Leaders who operate from power inspire their people through vision, integrity, and alignment with deeper values.

---

27   Ibid.

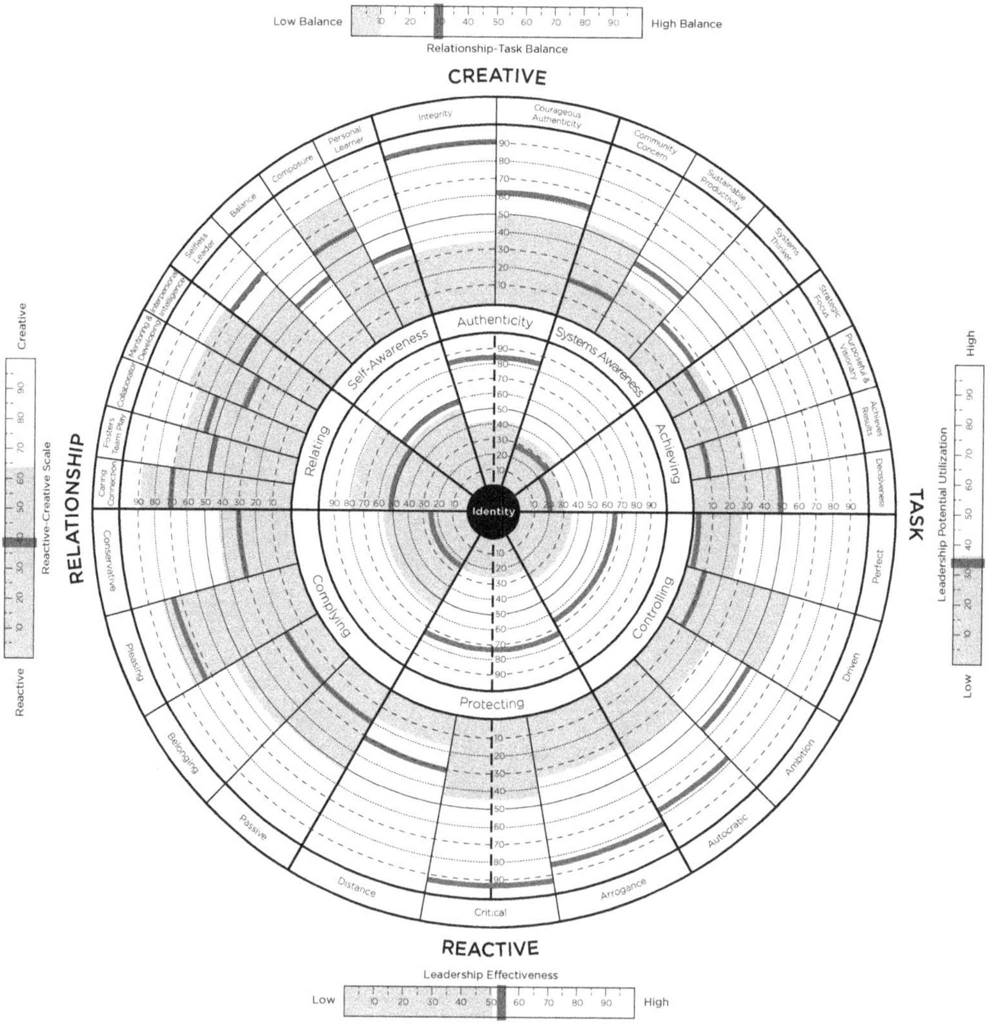
Low Balance
High Balance
Relationship-Task Balance
CREATIVE
Integrity
Courageous Authenticity
Community Concern
Sustainable Productivity
Systems Thinker
Strategic Focus
Purposeful & Visionary
Achieves Results
Decisiveness
Personal Learner
Composure
Balance
Selfless Leader
Interpersonal Intelligence
Mentoring & Developing
Collaborator
Fosters Team Play
Caring Connection
Authenticity
Self-Awareness
Systems Awareness
Relating
Achieving
Identity
Complying
Controlling
Protecting
Conservative
Pleasing
Belonging
Passive
Distance
Critical
Arrogance
Autocratic
Ambition
Driven
Perfect
RELATIONSHIP
TASK
REACTIVE
Creative
Reactive
Reactive-Creative Scale
High
Low
Leadership Potential Utilization
Leadership Effectiveness

Force represents something fundamentally different. It relies on position, control, competence, and compliance driven by fear—"boots on the neck." It comes from the leader's personal need for safety, security, and validation of identity. And while force may deliver results, often quickly, over time it diminishes trust, increases turnover, and sucks the life out of everyone involved—including (and especially) the leader themselves.

I know this burden intimately because I was that leader who led by force. A big part of my journey was discovering how exhausting it is to always be vigilant and deal with people tiptoeing around me, never feeling like they could be honest with me. Trust me when I tell you, force wears you down. The key insight that helped me finally shed this burden was recognizing that, in the end, power is really the absence of identity, while force is all about *you*. If your leadership is centered on your identity—your need to be right, to control, to be liked—that's a good sign you're operating from force. When your leadership is focused on a purpose beyond yourself, that's when you access genuine power.

THE THREE REACTIVE STYLES

The Buddhist tenet that "identity is a prison" directly connects to these ideas about power and force. Force is fundamentally rooted in our attachments to whom we think we are, how we think others should see us, and what we believe we need to protect or achieve. These attachments become the burdens that keep us from accessing true power and reaching our full potential. This can be especially destructive in leadership, where we lean into our defensive identities so hard that they become a sort of prison, limiting our effectiveness and draining our energy.

The three reactive styles we explored earlier—Complying, Protecting, and Controlling—each create their own kind of prison, representing a different manifestation of force-based leadership. What they have in common is that each of these identities, and the success strategies that once served us, wind up limiting and, many times, even canceling out our potential, locking us into patterns we can't escape. Aesop's fable "The Bat, the Bramble, and the Seagull" illustrates this beautifully while also reminding us that these patterns of behavior are as old as humanity itself.

The Bat, the Bramble, and the Seagull
—Aesop's Fables

Once upon a time, a Bat, a Bramble Bush, and a Seagull decided to start a business together. Each contributed something different: The Bat borrowed money from others to invest, the Bramble Bush supplied various fabrics and clothes, and the Seagull contributed a supply of lead. They loaded everything onto a ship and set sail.
Unfortunately, a terrible storm hit and sank their ship with all their goods. Though they survived and made it to shore, the experience changed them forever.

From that day on, the Bat only came out at night, afraid to face the people he'd borrowed money from. The Seagull spent its days flying over the ocean, constantly diving into the water searching for its lost lead. And the Bramble Bush began grabbing onto the clothes of anyone who walked by, desperately hoping to recover some of its lost fabrics.[28]

---

28 Aesop, "The Bat, the Bramble, and the Seagull," in *Aesop's Fables*, trans. V. S. Vernon Jones (Heinemann, 1912), 78.

This fable perfectly captures the three reactive styles identified in the Leadership Circle—ways we force rather than lead. The Bat represents the Protecting style, hiding away to avoid vulnerability and confrontation; the Bramble embodies the Complying style, grasping at relationships (symbolized by clothes) that pass by; and the Seagull illustrates the Controlling style, endlessly searching for and striving to recover what was lost through sheer determination and will. These reactive styles all represent success strategies that begin as strengths but become burdens when you rely on them instead of learning or growing beyond them.

I believe it's important that we invest the time to understand these success strategies because every leader brings one into their adult life. The leadership journey involves recognizing how and why these strategies once worked for you, how they now cancel you out, and what you need to do to grow beyond them. Let's look at them one at a time.

THE COMPLYING STYLE: STRENGTH OF HEART

The Complying style begins as a genuine strength—valuing relationships and connection. Leaders with this pattern typically developed social currency early in life. These are the people who were popular in high school—maybe they were elected student council president or prom queen. They learned from these experiences that to be safe, secure, and worthwhile in the world, they need to be likable and approachable in the eyes of others. This is an effective success strategy that serves these people well. We eagerly hire individuals with these qualities, and when they demonstrate them consistently, we promote them.

The challenge emerges when a person who needs to be likable finds themselves promoted into leadership. Suddenly, Mr. or Ms. Nice

Guy is in charge of other people and responsible for their performance. Imagine the struggle when they need to deliver difficult feedback to a direct report. That feedback gets filtered through their need to be liked, which means that, at best, it gets watered down, and at worst, it's never delivered at all. The strength of likeability becomes a limitation that prevents necessary truth-telling and holds everyone—the leader, their direct report, their organization—back.

Compliant people tend to view power as something to give away to serve and cement their relationships. They experience power as something to be distributed rather than held, often deferring to other people's needs and opinions at the expense of their own authority. They're skilled diplomats—they excel at creating harmony—but they struggle to take a stand in situations in which they might appear unlikeable. This power-diffusing tendency stems from their core belief that their value comes from connection and approval.

Just as the Bramble desperately clutches at every passing garment, hoping to recover what was lost, people who use the Complying style tend to grasp at relationships indiscriminately, measuring their success by how well they're liked rather than by the outcomes they create. Their fear of rejection leads them to surrender at the moment when decisive leadership is most needed.

THE PROTECTING STYLE: STRENGTH OF MIND

One of the gifts of the protected mind is discernment—these individuals have the ability to size up a situation at arm's length, dispassionately, and frequently be right about it. That's because the Protecting style is all about valuing competency and intelligence. These are the people who excel academically, who got perfect SAT scores, who led the honor society, and who had their pick of Ivy League schools. Their experience taught them that to be safe, secure, and worthwhile, they need to be smart and competent in the eyes of others. Like the Complying style, this strategy serves them well into adulthood. Who wouldn't want to hire a brilliant problem-solver who has the answer to almost any question?

The challenge arises when someone identified with their own brilliance is promoted into leadership. They struggle to develop competency in their people because they need to be the smartest person in the room—how can anyone else possibly solve the problem? Isn't their genius what got them there in the first place? So, they overedit and overcriticize other people's ideas, which cancels out their effectiveness as leaders.

When it comes to power, people with the Protecting style sometimes position themselves at a distance from it—they may analyze power structures but hesitate to participate fully in them. This standoffish relationship with power stems not from a lack of ambition but from fear that direct engagement might expose places where they're vulnerable or (gasp!) inadequate, threatening their carefully constructed identity as the smart and competent one. Just as the Bat retreated to the shadows to avoid confronting creditors, the Protecting style leads many brilliant people to retreat to the safety of analysis rather than risk the messy, imperfect work of wielding power authentically.

THE CONTROLLING STYLE: STRENGTH OF WILL

Much like the Complying and Protecting styles, the Controlling style begins as a valid success strategy—the drive to achieve and accomplish. Think of the high school athlete scoring touchdowns on Friday nights to standing ovations or the salesperson blowing past their quota quarter after quarter. From these experiences, they learn that to be safe, secure, and worthwhile, they need to be winning in the eyes of others.

This success strategy serves controlling types well in their careers. Everyone wants to hire a winner—for their drive and for the results they achieve—so we do, and the more they win, the higher we promote them. But once they make it to leadership, a person who identifies with scoring all the touchdowns might struggle to pass the ball to the next person. What if they drop it? What if they can't make it down the field as far? People using the Controlling style believe other people's failures reflect on them, so they micromanage, overcontrol, work too hard, and refuse to share responsibility.

When it comes to power, as you might imagine, people with the Controlling style welcome it and often wield it with some degree of intensity. They revel in their power (which is actually force in the Controlling style) because they see it as their primary tool to achieving the results they're after. So, their relationship with power is direct and unambiguous—more, please. They believe in taking charge, making decisions, and driving outcomes through sheer force of will. This need to concentrate power comes from their core belief that their worth comes from achievement and visible success.

Just as the Seagull relentlessly searches for its lost treasure, leaders stuck in the Controlling style are constantly scanning their environment for opportunities to demonstrate capability and tangible metrics to prove their success. Their fear of failure leads them to tighten their grip on power when empowering their people would often create better or more lasting results.

All three of these reactive styles, while beginning as strengths, can calcify into burdens that limit leadership effectiveness. They represent the bottom half of the Leadership Circle—force-based approaches that drain energy and restrict impact.

CREATIVE

REACTIVE

RELATIONSHIP

TASK

Traveling light means recognizing these patterns and beginning to move past them, not by rejecting them outright but by expanding beyond the limiting identities built around our strengths. Remember, human beings have had success strategies since Aesop's time, which means there's nothing wrong with you. The key is not eliminating your natural tendencies; it's learning to spot them and expanding beyond them.

FROM IDENTITY TO AWARENESS: WHEN YOUR REACTIVE STYLE GETS TRIGGERED

Whichever reactive style you identify with—Complying, Protecting, or Controlling—leadership is guaranteed to put you in situations that trigger your particular pattern. Know going in that these triggers aren't failures or weaknesses; they're predictable responses based on your success strategy.

If you use the Complying style, you'll get triggered when your relationships feel threatened. If you use the Protecting style, you'll get triggered when your competence is questioned. If you use the Controlling style, nothing will drive you crazier than your path to personal achievement getting blocked in some way.

Again, what distinguishes great leaders isn't the absence of these triggers—we all have them. It's their capacity to recognize and manage them effectively. Every leader faces moments when their reactive style flares up—that's just being human. The differentiator is what happens next.

When a reactive style gets triggered, if the leader doesn't know how to recognize or manage that trigger, there's an immediate cost. The compliant leader will back away from necessary conflict. The protected leader will withdraw into judgment and analysis. The controlling leader will micromanage even more. Each reaction stems from the leader's attempt to restore safety and security in the only way they know how—by doubling down on the very pattern that now limits them.

This is why awareness is the essential first step to traveling lighter. When you can recognize your reactive pattern when you're triggered, you create space to make a choice rather than react automatically.

DEVELOPING AWARENESS OF REACTIVE TRIGGERS

If you look at the top half of the Leadership Circle on the left side under "Relating," you'll see *awareness* listed as a key competency. Self-awareness is a superpower. It's important to develop the capacity to observe yourself and be realistic about feedback. The best leaders are feedback-seeking individuals—actively looking for input from others on their blind spots and impact.

This is why 360-degree assessments are so important and why joining a peer group is so valuable. You need feedback to become fully aware of what's inhibiting you and what it's costing you. Awareness is always the first step toward traveling lighter. Once you have it, you can begin working to counteract your reactive style.

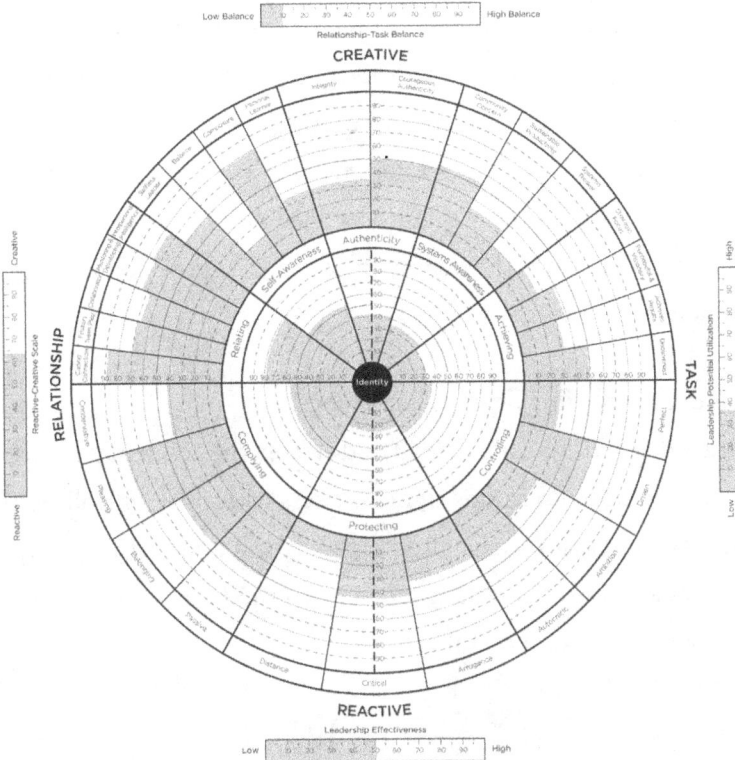

WORKING WITH YOUR REACTIVE STYLE: PRACTICAL APPROACHES

Since the reactive styles are different, each one requires a specific approach to develop new capacities and travel lighter.

For the Complying Style (Relating)

Start by practicing giving truthful, specific feedback to just one or two people. This directly challenges your need to be liked while building your capacity for courageous authenticity. When leaders with the Complying style learn that they can speak difficult truths while still maintaining their connection to others, they access a new level of leadership power.

For the Protecting Style (Thinking)

Go "three questions deep" in conversations, as we discussed in a previous chapter. This develops an attitude of curiosity that counterbalances your tendency to know it all. Those using the Protecting style overvalue their own brilliance and competency, believing they know the answers. By asking deeper questions, they discover new information that actually improves the quality of their decisions—something they genuinely value.

For the Controlling Style (Achieving)

Practice delegation. This directly addresses the tendency to believe that only you can do things right. Leaders with the Controlling style must learn to trust others with responsibility and resist the urge to micromanage. Effective delegation lightens their load while developing capacity in their team members.

THE ROLE OF COMMUNITY IN TRAVELING LIGHT

Traveling light does not mean traveling alone—pilgrims on the Camino find support and recognition from their fellow travelers, and leaders also need communities in which they can be seen and supported on their journey. I'm not just talking about simple encouragement, nor am I talking about other people providing the solutions to your problems. I'm talking about the power of being *witnessed* in both your struggles and your growth.

We discussed compliments and acknowledgments in a previous chapter, but this concept of witnessing also deserves attention. I've noticed that effective peer groups, particularly my Vistage groups, practice this powerful form of presence. Witnessing occurs when you are simply present for another person's journey from a place of knowing and acceptance. It's neither a compliment nor an acknowledgment. It's a way of being with someone that communicates, "I see you." I've watched leaders tackle incredibly difficult challenges over long periods, and while they carry the weight without complaint, they want to be witnessed in their journey. When this happens, it's like fuel in the engine—it gives them the energy to keep going.

Witnessing someone going through something difficult is a profound leadership skill. And no, it doesn't need to cross HR boundaries or violate professional norms. It's simply being there for each other from a place of shared journey and communicating that "We're all fellow leaders. We've all traveled this path. I know what you're experiencing." This quiet act of witnessing is one of the most beautiful things I observe in effective leadership peer groups, which is why I strongly encourage you to find one.

ESSENTIAL DISTINCTIONS: CLARIFYING WHAT MATTERS

One way a leadership peer group helps us travel light is by providing perspective on what really matters. When fellow leaders witness our journey, they can help us see distinctions we might miss on our own— distinctions that clarify which burdens are necessary for the road ahead and which can be left behind. Making these essential distinctions helps leaders focus their energy where it matters and release what doesn't. These key distinctions can transform how we approach leadership.

KEY LEADERSHIP DISTINCTIONS

- **Habits of Thinking/Patterns of Behaving**

  Leadership development requires awareness of both our mental models and our habitual behaviors. Traveling light means recognizing these habits and patterns so we can choose differently.

- **Speed Versus Effectiveness**

  Nearly every CEO I've coached values speed, yet what they truly need is effectiveness. Slowing down to move with intention often produces better results than rushing forward without clarity.

- **Stress Versus Pressure**

  Pressure comes when you face a significant deadline that you know how to meet. Stress happens when you face the same deadline without knowing how to proceed. Recognizing this distinction helps leaders address the real issue rather than just feeling overwhelmed.

- **Technical Versus Adaptive Challenges**

  As we discussed previously, technical challenges can be solved with existing knowledge and skills, whereas adaptive challenges require new learning, experimentation, and thinking outside established patterns. Leading through adaptive challenges demands what the Leadership Circle calls a creative mind—the ability to think beyond constraints and certainty.

- **The Responsibility To Versus The Responsibility For Distinction**
  Many leaders burden themselves by taking responsibility for things beyond their control—particularly others' emotional responses. As a leader, you're responsible for telling the truth respectfully, setting others up for success, and providing the necessary tools. You are not responsible for others' emotional reactions or attitudes.

- **Loyalty Versus Performance and Opportunity**
  Organizations typically begin with a loyalty-based culture in which heroic efforts are valued and rewarded. As they scale, they must evolve toward a performance and opportunity culture. This doesn't mean abandoning loyalty as a value but expanding its definition and preventing it from overshadowing performance.

- **Attention Versus Intention**
  This last distinction is particularly important. Someone once told me, "We do not suffer from attention deficit disorder. We suffer from *intention* deficit disorder." Most leaders believe they struggle with focus because they jump from task to task and are constantly distracted. But the real issue is a lack of clarity about what truly matters—an *intention* deficit.

When you're clear about what you're trying to accomplish and why it's important, your attention naturally follows it. Most leaders I work with don't do a good enough job of clarifying their intentions before diving into action, which brings us back to the difference between speed and effectiveness. To be truly effective, you must slow down and think about why something matters to you before directing your attention toward it.

THE POWER OF QUESTIONS: FOR THE PURPOSE OF WHAT?

If intention is so crucial to traveling light, how do we clarify our intentions when the leadership landscape is so complex? This is when the power of questions becomes essential. The right questions act as tools that help us strip away confusion and reconnect with what truly matters. And one of the most important questions I've developed in my work with leaders is simply, "For the purpose of what?"

When conversations veer off track or decisions become muddled, this question brings us back to intention. Back to making the main thing the main thing. Too often, we lose sight of our purpose when we feel ourselves getting overburdened. This question reconnects us with our intention—what are we truly trying to accomplish here? Here are two other related questions that help leaders travel light:

- Is every action I take aligned with the main thing?
- What does success look like?

These questions prevent us from carrying unnecessary burdens of activity without purpose.

PRACTICING RELEASE: WHAT TO SET DOWN

Once you've clarified your intentions and asked the right questions, you're ready to move into the deliberate practice of setting down the things that no longer serve you. Traveling light isn't just theoretical—it's also practical. Here are concrete examples of burdens leaders can and should release:

- an unproductive employee

- a bad customer

- a once profitable but now unprofitable product or service

- technical debt

- self-talk about growth and how big the business should be

- the need to know it all

But beyond these specific examples lies a more fundamental burden that deserves special attention: outdated knowledge.

LEARNING, UNLEARNING, AND RELEARNING

In his book *Future Shock*, Alvin Toffler famously said, "The illiterate of the 21st century will not be those who cannot read or write, but those who cannot learn, unlearn, and relearn."[29]

This echoes Darwin's insight that "It is not the strongest or fastest of the species that survives, it is the one most adaptable to change."[30]

And perhaps the most poignant quote is Eric Hoffer's observation that, "It is the learners who will inherit the future; the learned will find themselves wonderfully suited to a world that no longer exists."[31]

These three thinkers are all basically saying the same thing—that one of the heaviest burdens leaders carry is their outdated knowledge, approaches that worked for them in the past that no longer serve in the present. Traveling light means holding onto knowledge loosely

---

29 Alvin Toffler, *Future Shock* (Random House, 1970).

30 Leon Megginson, paraphrasing Charles Darwin, in "Lessons from Europe for American Business," *Southwestern Social Science Quarterly* 44, no. 1 (1963).

31 Eric Hoffer, *Reflections on the Human Condition* (Harper & Row, 1973).

enough that you can adapt when circumstances change. This ability to learn, unlearn, and relearn is perhaps the most important tool in our journey toward traveling light as leaders.

PRACTICAL TOOLS FOR TRAVELING LIGHT

Even when we recognize what weighs us down, the actual practice of letting go can be a challenge. The following tool kit offers various approaches—from delegation to deliberate practice—that can help you transform awareness into action.

- **Delegation and Critical Thinking**

  Getting tasks off your plate and onto someone else's is one of the most powerful ways to travel light. It's not about abdicating responsibility but about distributing the work in ways that leverage the strengths of your team. Teaching others to think for themselves creates independence and reduces the burden on leaders to solve every problem. This requires deliberate practice but yields exponential returns.

- **Upfront Agreements**

  Clarifying expectations at the beginning prevents the need to redo work later. Clear agreements reduce misunderstandings, conflicts, and the energy drain of ambiguity.

- **The Extraordinary Leader Model: Focusing on Strengths**

  The Extraordinary Leader model,[32] developed by Zenger and Folkman, parallels the top half of the Leadership Circle model we've

---

32 John Zenger and Joseph Folkman, *The Extraordinary Leader: Turning Good Managers into Great Leaders* (McGraw-Hill Education, 2009).

been discussing throughout this book. Their studies revealed that so-called extraordinary leaders significantly outperform average leaders by leveraging their strengths rather than focusing on fixing their weaknesses. Too many leaders exhaust themselves trying to be good at everything, when science has proven that developing a few standout strengths creates much more impact. While it's important to build your capacity in areas where you're weaker—something we'll get to a little later in the book—focusing too much time and energy on them is counterproductive and deprives your company and team of the best parts of you.

Zenger and Folkman introduced the 70-20-10 learning model, which aligns with our third Camino revelation (which we'll explore in a later chapter): The joy is in the walking. This model proposes that leadership development happens through

▫ 70 percent experiential learning (on-the-job challenges, stretch assignments),

▫ 20 percent social learning (mentoring, feedback, collaboration), and

▫ 10 percent formal training (workshops, books, leadership courses).

By focusing on natural strengths and real-world applications rather than remedial work on weaknesses, leaders can travel lighter, investing their energy where it will yield the greatest returns—in developing signature strengths through hands-on experience and meaningful relationships.

• The One Big Thing: Deliberate Practice

One of the most powerful tools I use with leaders is what I call the One Big Thing exercise. After reviewing the Leadership Circle's 360-degree feedback with a client, I ask them to identify one significant leadership behavior they want to develop. This approach draws on James Clear's concept of "deliberate practice" from his book *Atomic Habits*.[33]

We'll talk more about deliberate practice in chapter 6, but for now, know the process works like this.

• Define Your Leadership Development Plan

Following feedback, the leader creates an aspirational statement. For example, "I am the type of leader who ..." (is courageously authentic, delegates effectively, etc.)

• Clarify the *Why* and the *How*

I then guide them through a sequence of questions:

- Why is this important to you?

- What impact will this have on your organization?

- What behavior do you need to *start* doing (typically from the top half of the Leadership Circle)?

---

33 James Clear, *Atomic Habits: An Easy & Proven Way to Build Good Habits & Break Bad Ones* (Avery, 2018).

□ What behavior do you need to *stop* doing (typically from the bottom half)?

• **Commit to Focused Practice**

The leader commits to the deliberate practice of this one behavior.

The power of this approach is in its simplicity. Research now shows that focused, deliberate practice of a single leadership behavior cross-pollinates across the top half of the Leadership Circle.[34] Rather than trying to work on everything at once, leaders who travel light by focusing on *one big thing* that matters to them create ripple effects that expand their leadership capacity.

These are the two essential criteria for selecting this **one big thing**:

1. It must matter deeply to the leader—they need emotional energy and commitment behind it.

2. It should have a clear organizational benefit.

Beyond these criteria, there's no wrong choice. As I tell my clients, "You can't lose on this. It's deliberate practice toward a capacity that enhances how you show up as a leader."

THE POWER OF PAUSING: LISTENING TO DEEPER WISDOM

Among all the tools in the leader's journey to travel lighter, perhaps none is more powerful—yet more overlooked—than the act of

---

34   Lynn Harris, "5 Principles of Deliberate Leadership Practice," *LinkedIn,* May 27, 2021, https://www.linkedin.com/pulse/5-principles-deliberate-leadership-practice-lynn-harris/.

pausing. I'm not talking about inactivity; I'm talking about pausing as a purposeful tool that creates space for reflection, evaluation, and redirection. To truly set down our burdens, we have to stop moving long enough to recognize what we're carrying. David Whyte's poem "Sometimes" captures the transformative potential of this tool.

Sometimes
by David Whyte

Sometimes
if you move carefully
through the forest,
breathing
like the ones
in the old stories,
who could cross
a shimmering bed of leaves
without a sound,
you come to a place
whose only task
is to trouble you
with tiny
but frightening requests,
conceived out of nowhere
but in this place
beginning to lead everywhere.
Requests to stop what
you are doing right now,
and
to stop what you
are becoming

while you do it,

questions

that can make

or unmake

a life,

questions

that have patiently

waited for you,

questions

that have no right

to go away.

Whyte captures the essence of what happens when we truly pause as leaders. In the stillness, away from the constant motion of leadership demands, we encounter questions that have been waiting patiently for us—questions about what we're becoming, about the direction of our journey, about what truly matters. These aren't just any questions; they're the transformative kind that, as Whyte writes, "can make or unmake a life."[35]

The forest in Whyte's poem represents that rare space where we step away from our habitual paths of leadership. Just as the young people in the Native American tradition he references must find their way by listening deeply to nature, we as leaders discover our authentic direction by attending to the quiet wisdom that emerges only when we pause. Traveling light requires this willingness to be disturbed by the "tiny but frightening requests" that invite us to reconsider our journey.

Traveling light isn't something you do once and complete. Like the Camino itself, it's a daily practice of pausing to examine what you're carrying, asking if it serves your journey, and having the courage

---

35 David Whyte, *Everything Is Waiting for You* (Many Rivers Press, 2003).

to set down what no longer does. Each day offers new opportunities to shed unnecessary burdens—whether they're outdated success strategies, limiting beliefs, or responsibilities that belong to others.

The question isn't whether we're carrying burdens—we all are. The question is whether we're willing to recognize them and begin the practice of setting them down, one rock at a time.

REFLECTION QUESTIONS/EXERCISES

1. What outdated success strategies might be weighing you down in your current leadership role?

2. Which of the three reactive styles—Complying, Protecting, or Controlling—do you most identify with, and how might it be limiting your leadership effectiveness?

3. What is one burden you could set down immediately that would free up energy for more creative leadership?

4. How might your organization benefit if you traveled lighter as a leader?

5. What practice from this chapter could you commit to implementing this week to begin your journey toward traveling lighter?

As we've explored in this chapter, traveling light helps leaders move with greater agility and purpose, free from unnecessary burdens. But shedding these burdens is only one step in the leadership journey. What comes next is less about what we carry and more about how we see—how we perceive ourselves, our impact, and the inner dynamics that shape our leadership. In the next chapter, we turn toward the inner terrain: the spiritual journey of leadership and the self-awareness it requires.

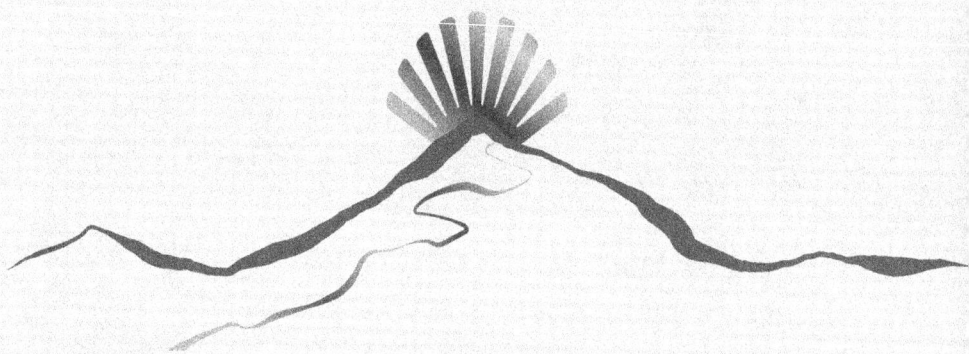

CHAPTER 5

THE SPIRITUAL JOURNEY— CULTIVATING SELF- AWARENESS

| *It's not what you look at that matters, it's what you see.* |

—HENRY DAVID THOREAU

Back in the dot-com days, I was the executive vice president of sales at a start-up. We were on the edge—completely out of money, trying to hit a subscription number that would unlock our next tranche of funding. I hadn't been paid in over eight weeks. I was newly divorced, juggling a mortgage and child support, and the pressure was beyond intense.

One afternoon, I was pacing the sales floor lost in thought and probably looking like a ghost. The president of the company pulled me aside and said, "Pete, what the hell is going on?"

I started to unload on him—"Don't you see the pressure I'm under?"—but he cut me off.

"Go home," he said. "Get your head out of your ass. And don't ever walk into this building again without your game face on."

I went home furious. But a few hours into my solo tantrum, I realized he was right. My stress had become contagious. My face was telling the team we were already out of business. That day, I learned something I've never forgotten: *Leaders bring the weather.* Your internal state creates the climate for everyone around you. If you don't know what's going on inside of you, you're going to send signals you don't mean to send—and people will interpret them faster than you can explain them.

What I didn't realize then—but have come to understand over time—is that what I was really learning in that moment was the foundation of a much deeper leadership truth. And it came into full focus years later, walking across the Meseta on the Camino de Santiago. That's where the second Camino revelation hit me: Travel with soft eyes.

WHEN THE PATH TURNS INWARD

After the challenges of the physical stage—with its steep ascents, rugged paths, and the body's protests against the daily long-distance walking—pilgrims enter a dramatically different landscape: the Meseta.

This vast, open plain of central Spain stretches seemingly endlessly before you, a sea of wheat fields rippling in the breeze under an enormous sky—at least that's what I saw in the heat of August, when I was there. While there were still the physical demands associated with walking fifteen or twenty miles a day, the nature of the challenge shifted. The difficulty was no longer navigating the terrain but confronting the monotony—the mental challenge of walking hour after hour through the same, unchanging landscape.

This transition from the mountains to the Meseta parallels the journey of leadership development. After mastering the initial challenges and basic skills of the physical phase, leaders enter a phase of deeper reflection and personal growth—a spiritual phase. The wide-open spaces invite pilgrims to turn inward, just as developing leaders must begin to explore their inner landscape—examining their motivations, values, and impact on others. This stage is about cultivating self-awareness and developing a deeper understanding of our purpose and potential.

In the early stages of the Camino, every pilgrim learns the importance of watching the path, looking for signs to make sure they're on the right route. This focus keeps you safe, but it also narrows your awareness. You miss the sweeping vistas, the ancient oak trees, the distant villages rising from the hillsides. You miss the context that gives your journey meaning.

On the Meseta, that shifted for me. I would get into a walking cadence—one foot in front of the other, one pole in front of the other, breathing in, breathing out. Sometimes I would realize I'd been walking for hours without even noticing the time pass. That cadence opened up a different kind of awareness. The Meseta doesn't demand your attention in the same way the mountains do. It invites you to notice your own inner terrain—your habits of mind, your emotional patterns, your defaults. And once you see them, you start asking better questions. Not just "What do I need to do next?" but also "Why do I keep doing it that way?" and "Where is that coming from?"

In many ways, this takes us back to the inner landscape of leadership—territory we began to explore in earlier chapters. But here, in this stage of the Camino, we go deeper. We begin the shift from reaction to reflection.

THE MOST IMPORTANT RELATIONSHIP

One of the biggest shifts leaders experience as they advance in their careers is that their job becomes increasingly relational—after all, leadership is a relational skill. At the entry levels of management, technical expertise and task proficiency will help you rise through the ranks. But as you start to climb higher, the quality of your relationships takes precedence. Leaders know this, and many focus extensively on how they relate to others—their communication style, their approach to delegation, their ability to influence and inspire their team. Unfortunately, far fewer pay attention to how they relate to themselves.

And yet, self-awareness is a cornerstone of relational leadership. Studies show that while most people believe they're self-aware, only 10 to 15 percent actually are.[36] That gap matters. Leaders who develop internal clarity are better equipped to lead authentically, build trust, and adapt in complex environments.[37]

Susan Scott, whom we met in a previous chapter, noted that, "We are always in conversations with ourselves, and sometimes those conversations involve others." This observation cuts to the heart of what makes great leaders effective—the most important relationship in your life is the one you have with yourself. That relationship—the internal narratives we embrace, the emotions we resist or give in to, the assumptions we make that ultimately drive our decisions—forms the foundation for all other leadership relationships.

When you're unaware of your internal landscape, you become a prisoner to it. Your unexamined beliefs drive your behavior. Your unacknowledged emotions color your perceptions. Your default thinking patterns limit your options. Cultivating self-awareness means learning

---

36 Tasha Eurich, "The Double-Edged Sword of Self-Awareness in Leadership," *Psychology Today*, September 29, 2024, https://www.psychologytoday.com/us/blog/the-clarity/202409/the-double-edged-sword-of-self-awareness-in-leadership.

37 Tasha Eurich, *Insight: The Surprising Truth About How Others See Us, How We See Ourselves, and Why the Answers Matter More Than We Think* (Crown Business, 2017).

to observe these internal forces without judgment—gaining a clearer understanding of what makes you *you*.

This is where we start to work with success strategies. Remember, these aren't strengths—they're strategies: the things you believe you need to do or be to stay safe, gain approval, or maintain control, even after they no longer serve you. They're often deeply ingrained, and they usually operate outside of conscious awareness. But once you see them and recognize them for what they are, you can begin to make different choices.

That's what self-awareness gives you: space to choose. Instead of being driven by the script, you start to question it. Instead of reacting from a triggered place, you pause. You gain perspective on yourself. And that's what allows everything else to change.

RECOGNIZING STRENGTHS AND LIMITATIONS

Part of self-awareness is recognizing what drives you, what you're good at, and yes, where you could use a little help. I'm infinitely curious, and I've learned a lot about myself through personality assessment tools, such as the Enneagram, the Predictive Index, and StrengthsFinder. There are other assessments too, and they all provide valuable information. But here's the key thing: They merely reveal data points. They're not the full truth. They give me something to get curious about or help illuminate something I had a sense of but couldn't articulate, but that's the extent of their power.

Still, seeing these data points grouped together and explained through a scientific framework can be incredibly useful in understanding how you're made up as a human being. In order to conduct any sort of leadership development, you need to know what you're working with—and one area where these tools are particularly helpful is in identifying where you need to build capacity. Because I guarantee there's an area where you do. Every assessment on every leader I've worked with has shown that wherever there's a strength, there's usually a corresponding area where they're not as capable. No one is equally good at everything.

For example, the Predictive Index—a behavioral assessment that measures workplace drives and motivations—tells me I have a "high A," or dominance, drive, meaning I value initiative and freedom of action. I like doing my own thing, my own way. The flip side is that I'm not naturally the best collaborator. I prefer being independent. However, if I truly want to be effective as a leader, I've learned that there are times when I have to engage with others—especially in big decisions and initiatives.

It's not my strong suit; I don't particularly like doing it, and I had a lot of self-talk about it:

"This is slowing me down."

"I'll never get this done if I have to wait for so-and-so."

If you don't understand the implications of your type, you might have similar conversations with yourself when confronted with your weaker points. Trust me, they won't be helpful. What is helpful is understanding that your weak points don't represent some fatal character flaw—they're just another data point. And that data point is sending you a simple message: Put some effort into valuing and building that leadership capacity.

You can learn how to do the thing you don't like or aren't good at. It might not be your strength, but you can plug in long enough to accomplish the task.

I know it works because I did it. And while it's still not my favorite thing to do, I discovered that if I involved others in the right way, I could gather incredible information that would help me make more effective decisions. In the end, for me, it came down to the speed versus effectiveness distinction we talked about in the last chapter.

Sometimes, what you're focused on is less important than what you're inadvertently sacrificing to get it. That's why it's essential to recognize the value of those capabilities you're missing and where they might be important. Once you're aware of where you need help, you can develop the capacity to be just good enough to deploy that capability when necessary—and then return to your natural strengths.

Having this baseline understanding of your strengths and limitations creates a foundation for self-aware leadership. When you recognize your natural tendencies and blind spots, it helps you move beyond your default perspective. You learn to compensate for your limitations while leveraging your strengths—all in service of more effective leadership.

The Predictive Index, for instance, helps you understand your drives—the internal motivations that shape how you work, communicate, and respond to your environment. Those drives aren't everything. If a client were to come to me and say they can't do something because it doesn't correspond with one of their drives, my response would be, "I don't care what your drives are; you still have a definition of leadership that has to be accomplished regardless of your natural tendencies."

But that doesn't mean the assessment isn't useful. When you see how you're naturally wired, of course you want to play to those strengths. But what's more important is gaining an understanding of your weaknesses, so you can develop the capacity to perform those tasks at least well enough.

WHAT GETS IN THE WAY

If self-awareness is so foundational, why don't more leaders invest in it? Why do so many people—even smart, experienced executives—stay stuck in their old patterns?

Because self-awareness is uncomfortable. It requires slowing down. It forces us to confront things we'd rather avoid. And most of all, it challenges the identity we've spent years reinforcing. Success strategies become invisible. We confuse our wiring with who we are. We stop being curious about our inner game and just start running it.

Here are ten of the most common obstacles I see that get in the way of developing self-awareness.

1. **Fear of Facing the Truth**

   Some leaders avoid self-reflection because they're terrified of what they might find. The potential for uncomfortable revelations can feel more threatening than staying as a limited version of themselves.

2. **Ego and Defensiveness**

   The ego doesn't like to admit weakness. It constructs narratives to protect our self-image, creating blind spots that block genuine insight.

3. **Lack of Time to Reflect**

   In hyperconnected, always-on environments, leaders get caught in constant motion. Busyness becomes a shield against deeper questions.

4. **Dependence on External Validation**

   When your identity is tied to how others perceive you, self-awareness gets filtered through the need to look good rather than to grow.

5. **Blind Spots and Cognitive Biases**

Unconscious patterns distort how we interpret our actions and motives. You can't see the lens you're looking through—unless you know to look for it.

6. **Emotional Discomfort**

Facing negative emotions takes courage. It's easier to suppress or ignore feelings than to explore what they're trying to teach us.

7. **Fixed Mindset**

If you believe your personality is fixed, growth feels impossible. Why look inward if nothing can change?

8. **Social and Cultural Conditioning**

We're shaped by family, culture, and society—often in ways we never examine. Those early narratives can drown out what's true for us now.

9. **Avoidance of Feedback**

Some leaders sidestep feedback to avoid criticism, but this avoidance cuts them off from the raw material of growth.

10. **Lack of Mindfulness**

If you're not paying attention to your present thoughts, emotions, and behaviors, you can't reflect on them. Awareness can't happen without attention.

These barriers aren't personal failings. They're just the terrain. The point isn't to eliminate them all—it's to become aware of which ones are operating in you. That's where self-awareness matters most. It helps you to stay curious in the face of discomfort. To ask better questions. To widen the lens just enough to see clearly—and, when it matters most, to choose differently.

BRINGING THE WEATHER

Self-awareness isn't just about understanding our strengths and limitations. It's also about moving beyond the beliefs and assumptions we've formed over time. That's critical, because beliefs aren't just ideas we hold—they're commands to our nervous system. They shape how we perceive and interact with the world, whether we realize it or not.

At the beginning of this chapter, I shared the story of how I learned an uncomfortable truth—that leaders bring the weather. Just like actual weather creates the conditions in which everything else must function, a leader's internal state—especially their emotional state—creates the climate for the entire organization.

Think of your internal operating system like a computer's core programming. A system can only handle as much complexity as the operating system it is running on. It's the same with leadership. If you're operating from what we've been calling a reactive (Anderson), Level 3 (Collins), or expert mind (Kegan), you'll respond to complexity very differently—and much less effectively—than if you're operating with a creative, Level 5, or achievement mind. And when it comes to emotional regulation, the difference is dramatic.

We've already explored the distinction between having emotions and emotions having you. That difference becomes even more important when you consider that a leader's emotional state ripples outward. When emotions have a leader—when the leader is reactive, stressed, and anxious—that emotional energy spreads to their team, whether they say anything or not. But when a leader can hold their emotions—experience them without being controlled by them—they create stability. They bring calm. They bring clarity. This is never more important than during times of crisis.

As I write this, I'm witnessing another black swan event unfold in the DC area, where my Vistage practice is based. Budget constraints have suddenly led to canceled government contracts, leaving businesses in turmoil. It feels like the COVID-19 pandemic all over again for this segment of the community—they're completely shut down.

In my Vistage meetings this week, I've heard from members whose long-term contracts were canceled overnight. I'm watching longtime members lay off employees they've worked with for fifteen years. People they care about. The uncertainty is thick, and nobody knows when—or if—stability is coming back.

A critical part of our conversations has been about how leaders show up in front of their people during this kind of disruption. Because their teams are watching. They're reading the emotional weather, even if no one's saying anything out loud. The leader's internal state becomes the external climate.

In moments like these, self-awareness isn't a luxury. It's not extra. It's vital. It's what allows leaders to regulate their emotions, stay grounded, and make clearheaded decisions. That kind of presence stabilizes the organization. It gives people something to hold onto when everything else is going crazy. That's what my boss was talking about when he told me to get my head out of my ass and never walk into the office again without my game face on.

SHIFTING FROM REACTIVE TO CREATIVE

Of course, all of this only matters if you're willing to put in the work it takes to change. I've experienced this firsthand. One of the biggest shifts in my own leadership came when I started to understand the difference between speed and effectiveness.

You're probably familiar with NASCAR, where a bunch of professionals get in a high-performance, precision machine and drive it in traffic for several hours at around two hundred miles per hour. It's high performance at its most visceral. You can't even get on that track unless you can sustain that level of performance and intensity. And in the end, what separates the top performers—those who come in first, second, or third—from the rest of the pack comes down to about one or two miles per hour ... every lap.

That may not seem like much, but it's the critical differential. And when you take the engines back into the shop and break them down, what contributes most to potential engine failure isn't speed—it's revolutions per minute (RPMs). How hard did the engine have to work to gain that extra mile per hour? To me, this is a powerful leadership metaphor. Can you increase your miles per hour while simultaneously lowering your RPMs? That's what I work on with my clients. That's what I work on with myself.

My own self-awareness journey was about shifting from the need to be right to the need to understand what's true. For a long time, I was getting a lot of feedback and pushback. People were arguing with me all the time, and I wasn't getting the results I wanted or needed. But I kept insisting on my position. I insisted I was right, and I was wedded to the need to be right.

It didn't happen all at once, but eventually I woke up and got over myself. I was so exhausted from trying it my way and holding on so tightly to being right. I don't think there was a single epiphany moment—I think it just occurred to me over time that the more important value wasn't being right but getting to the right outcome.

What was the truth of the situation? What was the *right* decision—not just *my* decision?

That was a developmental leap for me. My value system started to evolve—leadership became less about protecting my ego and more about finding clarity. My ego started to lose its grip on me, or maybe I lost my grip on it. Either way, it loosened.

And when that happened, my decision-making got better. I was more open. I listened more. I could integrate more information, especially when it came from someone who saw something I didn't.

I realized that being wrong wasn't some kind of indictment. It just meant I didn't have enough data yet. Somebody else had better information. And the moment I became willing to be wrong in service of the right decision, my miles per hour went up and my RPMs went down. It actually took stress out of my system.

Not always needing to be right gives you the freedom to consider more possibilities. It gives you permission to pause and shift perspective instead of defending your position out of habit. That's the move from being reactive to being creative. It's a real shift in consciousness, and it's something every leader eventually has to go through.

I can't tell you how many leaders I've worked with who struggle at this exact point—letting go of the need to be right and moving to the need to find the truth. But I've seen what happens when they make that shift. They get better results, and they get them with less stress. Just like I did.

GETTING CURIOUS ABOUT FEEDBACK

The most effective leaders I know want to know how they're landing, how they're being experienced, what's working, and what's not. So, they are feedback junkies. They don't just wait for the formal 360-degree feedback—they're asking questions, seeking feedback all the time.

For instance, they are saying, "Give me something. What are you seeing? How did that come across?"

They know it's not personal, it's information. They want the data because they know it helps them lead better. It's not about whether the feedback is right or wrong. It's about how it helps them understand their impact.

> **That's the key:** *Self-aware leaders understand that how they intend to come across isn't always how they're actually experienced. And unless someone tells them, they'll keep walking around assuming everything is fine.*

This is where tools, such as the 360-degree Leadership Circle Profile, or a peer group, such as Vistage, are so useful. They help bridge the gap between intention and perception. They show you how others experience you. And once you know that, you can begin to make intentional shifts. You can choose when to adapt, when to hold, and when to stretch.

That's not always easy. A lot of leaders struggle when feedback feels like criticism. They get defensive. I've seen it over and over again—and I've lived it.

My advice for a good first step is to pause. Just pause. Recognize the emotional reaction you're experiencing, then create a little space between the reaction and your response. That's a skill. It takes practice. But it's at the heart of every meaningful growth moment I've seen in my work.

Consider the leader who learns, through feedback, that they tend to avoid conflict. Maybe they've always told themselves they were just keeping the peace. But now they can see that in avoiding difficult conversations, they've actually been creating confusion, frustration, or even resentment on their team.

Armed with that self-knowledge, they can choose a different path. They can learn to engage in hard conversations instead of backing away. That doesn't happen without feedback. And it doesn't stick without self-awareness.

This is how real change happens—incrementally, one moment at a time. It's not about perfection. It's about developing the internal muscles to receive information, assess it honestly, and use it to grow.

WHY CHANGE IS SO HARD

Even with awareness and feedback, change can still feel impossible. And that's not because leaders don't want to grow. It's because something deeper is holding them in place—something they often can't see.

"Immunity to Change" is a concept developed by Robert Kegan and Lisa Lahey that explains why people struggle to change even when they're highly motivated.[38] They found that beneath every sincere commitment to grow, there's often a hidden, competing commitment—an unconscious belief or fear that works against the desired change.

These competing commitments are usually driven by big assumptions—deep, hidden beliefs about what will happen if we behave differently. They're like an internal immune system: protecting us from perceived threats but also preventing transformation.

Kegan and Lahey use a simple but powerful structure to help leaders map this out:

- **Improvement goal:** what you're trying to do differently
- **Current behaviors:** what you're actually doing instead
- **Hidden competing commitments:** the fears or protective instincts driving those behaviors
- **Big assumptions:** what you believe will happen if you don't uphold those hidden commitments

---

38 Robert Kegan and Lisa Lahey, *Immunity to Change: How to Overcome It and Unlock the Potential in Yourself and Your Organization* (Harvard Business Press, 2009).

Once you see it on paper, it's obvious. But until you do, that hidden layer runs the show.

There's a quote from Kegan and Lahey's *An Everyone Culture* that I come back to often:

> In an ordinary organization, most people are doing a second job no one is paying them for. Most people are spending time and energy covering up their weaknesses, managing other people's impressions of them, showing themselves to their best advantage, playing politics, hiding their inadequacies, hiding their uncertainties, hiding their limitations.
>
> Hiding. We regard this as the single biggest loss of resources that organizations suffer every day.[39]

That line hit me hard. Because I see it all the time.

Leaders are always doing a second job. In the reactive mind (Level 3), that second job is hiding. In the creative mind (Level 5), the second job becomes development—continuously growing the complexity of your own mind.

Immunity to Change gives us a map to make that shift. It surfaces the unconscious patterns that block transformation. Once you become aware of those assumptions, you can begin to challenge them—and that's when real change becomes possible.

STILLNESS, REFLECTION, AND THE JOURNEYMAN MINDSET

One thing I've noticed over the years is that every Level 5, highly creative leader I've worked with has some kind of practice that helps

---

39   Robert Kegan and Lisa Lahey, *An Everyone Culture: Becoming a Deliberately Developmental Organization* (Harvard Business Review Press, 2016).

them slow down and turn inward. It doesn't have to be meditation. For some people, it's a centering prayer. For others, it's movement— running, hiking, walking the dog. Or it's spending time in nature. The point is always the same: Create stillness. Create space. That's how you learn to hear yourself.

As I tell leaders all the time, you've got to close the door, put your feet on the desk, and give yourself time to think. I mean, actually close the door—no calls, no email, no meetings. You've got to step out of the swirl. That's not wasted time. That's where the real thinking happens. That's where pattern recognition happens. That's where you stop reacting and start seeing.

On the Camino, stillness didn't come from sitting behind a closed door—it came from those long stretches when the repetition of walking created just enough quiet in my head, allowing me to finally hear myself. No distractions. Just the rhythm of my steps and the space to think. And in that space, things began to settle.

That's why I talk about leaders as journeymen. It's not about mastery. It's about remaining in the process. It's about developing the complexity of your mind to meet the complexity of your challenges. That's what leadership is. It's about becoming the kind of person who doesn't just react—but reflects, adapts, and leads.

Leadership journeymen know they're not finished, ever, and that their journey continues with each new day. And that mindset doesn't just affect them—it ripples out to everyone around them. When leaders take the time to turn inward—to examine their assumptions, regulate their emotions, and develop their inner game—it shows up in how they lead others. They bring more calm, more clarity, and more direction. Their presence shifts the tone of the room. Their example gives others permission to grow, too. Their inner work becomes everyone else's outer environment.

The best leaders I know

- stay curious,

- embrace growth,

- reflect on experiences, and

- adapt to change.

Self-aware leadership increases resilience and adaptability. Leaders who acknowledge their own uncertainty during tough situations, yet confidently share their vision, build authentic trust. They create clarity and confidence in their teams. They help people navigate complexity with purpose. I tell my clients all the time: These moments—the COVID-19 pandemic, government shutdowns, budget freezes—are shaping moments. You'll look back on these and realize they were the times that grew you the most.

How do I know? Because my biggest growth happened during some of those shit storms.

And I've never met a leader who said otherwise.

REFLECTION QUESTIONS/EXERCISES

1. Where am I operating at high speed but high RPMs? What's driving that strain?

2. What default thinking patterns might be limiting my options as a leader?

3. How am I being experienced by others? What feedback have I heard recently—and how did I react to it?

4. What big assumptions might be keeping me from making a change I say I want?

5. When do I feel most grounded, clear, and fully present? How can I create more of that?

In the next chapter, we'll move from insight to integration, where daily practice becomes the path, shifting from breakthrough moments to rhythm, consistency, presence, and beauty in the everyday. Because the real journey of leadership isn't built on dramatic change. It's built one step at a time.

CHAPTER 6

THE JOY IS IN THE WALKING— EMBRACING THE DAILY PRACTICE OF LEADERSHIP

Find a place inside where there's joy, and the joy will burn out the pain. The vital force within you is the same as that which created the universe, and the vital force vitalizes.

—JOSEPH CAMPBELL

I was about six hours into one of those long, hot days on the Camino. My knees ached, flies buzzed around my head in slow circles, and the sun was beating down overhead. I'd slipped into a slump—not just in spirit but physically—head down, grinding my boots into the dust, feeling sorry for myself. I was just miserable.

Then I caught myself.

"Pick your head up," I said. "Look around."

I did. And what I saw was breathtaking—wide-open country, rolling hills, something wild and still and alive in the land. And I remembered, *You asked for this.*

That moment became one of the most important lessons I took from the Camino. Because I wasn't in danger, or lost, or in any more pain than what had become the norm. I was just in a hard moment—and I was choosing to carry it badly. And leadership has plenty of those hard moments.

The daily walk of a leader isn't dramatic most of the time. It's not all keynote speeches and the company-wide strategy rollouts. It's sitting with a direct report and having a difficult conversation about what's not going well. It's preparing for a board meeting you fully expect to be brutal. It's holding the line when no one's watching. It's walking into another day with a full calendar and making the choice to lead with clarity and compassion anyway and coming back the next day and doing it all again.

More than anything else, it's finding the joy in the process of doing those ordinary, everyday things. My Camino pilgrimage wasn't about that moment when I finally reached Santiago; it was about the process of getting there, even the painful parts. That's what prompted my third Camino revelation: The joy is in the walking.

This chapter is about that kind of walking. It's about the work leaders do, not once, but every single day. And it's about how the way you carry yourself in those ordinary, often repetitive moments has an extraordinary impact over time. It's all about the rhythm of the walk itself, the cadence of practice, and the quiet heroism of showing up and doing the work—again and again and again.

We've already established that leadership is not some destination to reach or summit to stand on. It's a path you walk every day. Great leaders don't rely on flashes of brilliance; what sustains them is rhythm. Practice. Honing their craft, not for perfection but for growth.

And here's what I've seen in working with hundreds of CEOs: It doesn't always come naturally. Every leader initially avoids whatever tasks they don't like doing or don't feel they're good at, focusing all their energy on what comes naturally. It's human nature. But the truly exceptional leaders are the ones who learn to get comfortable with discomfort—who recognize that the parts of leadership that challenge them most are precisely where their greatest growth potential lies.

Just as I had to lift my head on the Camino to see the beauty that surrounded me, leaders need to lean into their challenges to discover unexpected possibilities. It's there, inside those moments you'd rather avoid, that something wonderful can happen. And ultimately, if you're not willing to embrace these difficult aspects of leadership, you won't reach your Santiago—whatever that destination means to you.

David Whyte wrote, "The antidote to exhaustion is not rest. It's wholeheartedness."[40] In other words, joy doesn't come from the absence of effort. It comes from reconnecting with what matters— what drew you to this work in the first place. When leaders lose that connection, they're vulnerable to burnout. When they regain it, even briefly, it fuels their resolve.

That's why one of the most important roles I play as a coach is helping leaders return to their why. When the pressure gets high and the grind wears them down, I want to honor the exhaustion—but I also want to bring them back to the reasons they chose this path in the first place.

This chapter will explore how that reconnection happens through the daily walk, which includes one-to-ones, deliberate practice, compounding effort, rituals of reflection, and acts of leadership that may seem small in the moment but ultimately shape your culture, grow your capacity, and build trust.

---

40   Robert Whyte, *Crossing the Unknown Sea: Work as a Pilgrimage of Identity* (Riverhead Books, 2002).

FROM MINDSET TO PRACTICE: LEADERSHIP AS A DAILY RHYTHM

In the previous chapter, I described how, after reaching the Meseta on the Camino, I discovered something profound as I found myself settling into a natural rhythm—that a regular walking cadence somehow transformed my experience from exhausting to energizing.

Each morning, I would set out with a clear focus: that day's journey, not tomorrow's or next week's. I knew every day when I got out of bed that fifteen miles from then, my day would be done. It reminds me of Jim Collins's concept of the "20-Mile March."[41] Collins found that the most successful companies didn't make progress through dramatic leaps or heroic efforts. Instead, they committed to consistent forward movement—such as marching twenty miles every day regardless of conditions. They created clear performance markers and self-imposed constraints and maintained high consistency regardless of circumstances.

On the Camino, I broke down the five-hundred-mile journey into digestible daily segments—each with a beginning and an end. This daily rhythm created a compounding effect. By the time I was two-thirds through the pilgrimage, I knew exactly what to expect: "There's going to be a beginning and an end every day. There's going to be some soreness involved, and I'll be just fine." The confidence that comes from consistent practice allowed me to move beyond merely surviving each day (sometimes in complete misery) to actually experiencing the journey fully.

---

41   Jim Collins and Morten Hansen, *Great by Choice: Uncertainty, Chaos, and Luck— Why Some Thrive Despite Them All* (Random House Business Books, 2011).

That's when I began to experience what psychologist Mihály Csíkszentmihályi calls the "flow state"[42]—a condition of complete focus where time seems to stop. On the Camino, I would realize I had been walking for hours, lost in this state of immersive engagement. The prerequisites were simple but powerful: Commit fully to the task at hand, give it undivided attention, understand its purpose, and then dive in.

What's fascinating is how directly this translates to leadership. Leaders who thrive long term aren't the people who make occasional heroic efforts; they're the people who develop these consistent rhythms of engagement, reflection, and growth.

In my work with CEOs, I've found that one of the biggest barriers to this kind of flow is fragmented attention. Many leaders need permission to create uninterrupted blocks of time—to metaphorically close the door to distractions, as I mentioned in the previous chapter, and dive deeply into important work. Without this protected space away from the noise of the day-to-day, the flow state that enables our best thinking and most creative problem-solving is hard to achieve.

> Leaders who thrive in the long term understand that leadership isn't about isolated achievements but about the daily practice of showing up every day with intention.

The rhythm of leadership, like the rhythm of walking the Camino, is all about this kind of sustained presence. It's about finding a pace that allows you to notice what's happening around you while still moving steadily forward. As a leadership journeyman, your growth doesn't come from occasional breakthroughs but from the consistent cadence of practice—showing up day after day, bringing your full attention to the work, and allowing that rhythm to transform both you and your organization.

---

42   Mihály Csíkszentmihályi, *Flow: The Psychology of Optimal Experience* (Harper & Row, 1990).

DELIBERATE PRACTICE IN LEADERSHIP

Once you understand that leadership is a daily rhythm, the next question becomes: How do you make that rhythm productive? This is where the concept of deliberate practice becomes vital.

When researcher Anders Ericsson studied expert performers across various fields, he discovered that excellence isn't just about putting in time—it's about how you use that time.[43] It turns out that experts thrive when they engage in highly structured activities that have been specifically designed to improve performance in their domain. Ericsson discovered that real improvement begins with just twenty minutes a day of focused effort. For leaders, deliberate practice means following a simple but powerful three-step process.

DELIBERATE PRACTICE ESSENTIALS

1. Decide on a small subskill to practice.

2. Practice with 100 percent focus.

3. Get feedback and reflect.

This approach differs dramatically from how most leaders develop. Many default to what could be called *accidental practice*—handling situations as they arise, sometimes well and sometimes not so well, but without a structured approach to learning from those experiences.

What I've come to believe is that I'm a practitioner at heart. Leadership, to me, is a practice in the truest sense—such as meditation, or music, or any craft where you sit down and deliberately pay attention to something that builds your capacity to do it even better.

---

43   Anders Ericsson et al., "The Role of Deliberate Practice in the Acquisition of Expert Performance," *Psychological Review* 100, no. 3 (1993).

You're not trying to reach some end point. You're engaging with the work, again and again, because there's always something new to learn, always some dimension of your leadership to sharpen or stretch.

This approach aligns perfectly with Jim Collins's "20-Mile March" concept that I mentioned earlier. Consistency is the heart of sustainable productivity. It's not about short bursts of activity or heroics under pressure. It's about the ability to operate at a high level over time—to keep walking the twenty-mile march day after day, quarter after quarter. Sustainable productivity is what allows you to endure. It's not just surviving; it's producing value, solving problems, developing people, and doing it all without burning out.

Leaders often get promoted because they can deliver this kind of performance personally—they can self-regulate, focus, and perform at a consistently high level. But the real leap comes when they're asked to generate sustainable productivity across their team. That's instantly more complex. Because now it's not just about their habits, it's about their influence.

You can't control how others show up—but you can absolutely influence it. And good leadership has that kind of influence. The daily walk—delegation, one-to-ones, feedback, defining success clearly, showing you care—may involve soft skills, but they're also the exact tactics that drive sustainable productivity inside an organization. They're what turn individual output into team momentum.

And just as sustainable productivity is built on consistent execution, the same principle applies to leadership development. Rather than waiting for transformative moments or breakthrough insights, being a leadership journeyman means committing to small, consistent steps forward. It means viewing setbacks not as failures but as valuable feedback. Each challenge becomes an opportunity to learn and adjust in the next cycle of practice.

These small improvements create a ripple effect, building upon each other, creating momentum that eventually leads to significant growth. Just as my body adapted to the daily rigor of the Camino, leadership capacity expands through this consistent, focused practice.

The key is to be specific and realistic about what you're practicing. Don't try to boil the ocean by attempting to fix everything all at once. Instead, identify one leadership skill that, if improved, would have the greatest impact on your effectiveness. Direct your attention there, practice deliberately, seek feedback, reflect—and then watch as that focused energy ripples out.

SUSTAINING MOMENTUM

There are moments on any long journey when it feels impossible to take another step. On the Camino, I hit those walls more times than I'd like to admit—moments when my knees were screaming, my energy was depleted, and I questioned why I ever thought this ridiculous pilgrimage was a good idea. Leadership has those same moments of exhaustion and doubt, when the demands feel overwhelming and motivation evaporates. Those moments are when rituals and routines will get you through.

In my work with CEOs, many leaders initially resist the idea of structured reflection time. They're so focused on driving results that stepping back to assess their progress seems unnecessary. But just as I needed to periodically check my map and adjust my pace on the Camino, leaders need regular reflection to ensure they're on the right path.

This might take the form of a daily reflection practice—just ten to fifteen minutes at the beginning or end of your day to consider what went well, what could be improved, and what key decisions you made that impacted your team. Some leaders keep a leadership journal in which they track these insights, creating a record of their journey that they can review periodically to see patterns and progress.

DAILY LEADERSHIP REFLECTION QUESTIONS

1. What did I accomplish today?

2. What went well?

3. What would make it even better the next time?

4. Where did I hold back and why?

Weekly check-ins provide a broader perspective. Every Friday afternoon, take thirty minutes to evaluate the key leadership moments and learning points from the past week. How aligned were your decisions with your core values? What clear focus and intention will you bring to next week? This practice creates a natural rhythm of closure and reset that prevents the weeks from blending together.

Monthly planning is another ritual I strongly advocate for. Rather than letting each month unfold reactively, I plan my month in advance, identifying priorities, allocating time for strategic thinking, and making space for leadership development, personal restoration, and all the things I've determined I need to operate at my best. This way, I'm sure I'm driving my calendar rather than having my calendar drive me—something I strongly suggest to my coaching clients.

Communication routines are equally important for keeping the team engaged. Daily stand-ups, weekly recaps, and regular debriefs after significant projects help create a shared cadence that aligns everyone's efforts. The most effective format I've seen is a simple retrospective: What went well? What would make it better next time? These routines create structure and accountability, especially in peer group settings.

As I often remind my Vistage members, "We are not business people having human experiences; we are human beings having business experiences." Creating rituals that honor both dimensions is crucial.

I'm often asked about my own routines, and I'll admit that I could be better at some of these practices. For instance, reflective journaling is something I recommend but don't consistently do myself. However, I do plan my month in advance, maintain a gratitude practice, and have a breathing practice that grounds me.

The routine I think gets overlooked the most by leaders is celebrating small wins. Every leader I've ever worked with has needed to do this better. Research has proven that catching people getting it right, acknowledging progress, and marking milestones actually triggers the release of dopamine in the brain, which reinforces the behaviors that lead to success.[44] This isn't just feel-good psychology—it's neurochemistry that drives real-world performance.

The celebration of small wins is particularly important because the journey of leadership is long. Without pausing to recognize progress along the way, it's easy to lose heart or perspective. One of my big lessons on the Camino was to celebrate each day's walking rather than focusing only on getting where I was going. The leadership journeymen must learn to find joy and satisfaction in the daily practice of leadership, not just in reaching those major milestones.

But all of this—the reflection, the rhythm, the planning, the communication, the celebration—only works if it's embedded in a culture that supports it. You can do everything right as a leader and

---

44 Wolfram Schultz, "Dopamine Reward Prediction Error Coding," *Dialogues in Clinical Neuroscience* 18, no. 1 (2016): 23–32.

still find yourself pushing a boulder uphill if the people around you aren't also growing. That's why I'm such a strong believer in what Robert Kegan and Lisa Lahey call the Deliberately Developmental Organization, or DDO.

I introduced Kegan and Lahey's book *An Everyone Culture* in chapter 5. The book starts with this premise: Growth isn't extra. It's the job. Not just for you but for everyone. In a DDO, development isn't reserved for high-potential employees or handed off to HR. It's part of how the business runs. Everyone has a growth plan. Everyone is expected to stretch, and the organization supports them in doing so. Feedback and reflection aren't occasional—they're routine. These aren't soft skills. They're how performance becomes sustainable across time.

When I coach CEOs, I challenge them to go beyond personal development, bake this into the culture, and put it under their control. Make growth nonnegotiable—not in a harsh way, but in a way that says, "Your development matters. We're going to take it seriously, and so should you." One of the simplest and most effective ways I've found to build that culture is with a few direct questions that can be asked during a self-assessment exercise or with the help of a coach or mentor:

- What's a challenge you're facing right now that's going to stretch you?

- What are you doing to grow into it?

- Who else is in on it with you—who's tracking your progress and cheering you on?

- Why is this challenge worth it to you?

If a leader can answer those four questions out loud—and better yet, if their team can too—that's the sign of a healthy developmental culture. This kind of transparency isn't just useful, it's powerful. And in my experience, Vistage peer groups model this beautifully. Growth is out in the open. It's normal to talk about what you're working on, how you're working on it, and why it matters.

So ask yourself these questions:

- Does every person who reports to you have something they're actively working on?

- Do they know what the impact on the organization is?

- Are you part of the support system that helps them grow?

Because here's the truth: The leader's job isn't to do more. It's to grow the capacity of the organization to do more. And that can't happen if the growth stops with you. You can't scale a business unless you're scaling leadership. And you can't scale leadership unless the people around you are growing too.

And that brings us back to the daily walk and the real work of leadership that happens in the small, repeatable things you do every day.

THREE ESSENTIAL DAILY PRACTICES OF LEADERSHIP

A deliberately developmental culture doesn't build itself. It takes consistent, everyday effort—especially in how you lead. These three practices are the daily tools I come back to with every CEO I coach. They're straightforward, repeatable, and when done well, they create the conditions for growth.

Let's start with the one-to-one meeting.

1. **The One-to-One**

Most leaders conduct one-to-ones, but few do them well because they focus on transactional one-to-ones that concentrate on updates, tasks, and troubleshooting—the business of the day. They're necessary, but they don't move the needle on long-term growth. Transformational one-to-ones, on the other hand, are about development. The reason we're talking is to grow your capacity in the role. Those are the one-to-ones all leaders should be performing on a regular basis.

These conversations are about helping someone become a better version of themselves over time. They're structured and intentional, and they require the leader to show up as both an advocate and an accountability partner. You're there to help them grow—and to hold them accountable for owning that growth.

For this to work, the meetings have to be regular and nonnegotiable. They don't have to be weekly, but they do have to happen consistently. And most importantly, they need to be owned by the person receiving the one-to-one. That means they come prepared. I always begin by asking, "What's the most important thing we should be talking about today?" I tell them from day one, "I'll ask you this question every single time. Think about it ahead of time."

Often, especially early on, they'll come in with nothing. That's when I hold the line. "This is your one-to-one. How are you not prepared?" It's part of the rigor. It's uncomfortable sometimes, but if you hold space for that discomfort, something starts to shift. Eventually, they come in ready. They bring their development into the room. And when they do that, real transformation begins.

This is learned behavior for both sides. It's especially hard for leaders who operate from a reactive mindset—who don't want to make people uncomfortable or fear being seen as too tough. But leadership isn't about being liked. It's about showing up for the people you lead in a way that builds their belief in themselves. That takes structure. It takes repetition. It takes trust. And trust comes from showing consistent interest in who they are and who they're becoming.

If you do this long enough, something beautiful happens: They start to believe you're genuinely invested in them. And if you ask the right questions and shut up long enough to let them squirm, eventually they'll bring something real. You become a partner in their development. That's not just performance management—that's leadership.

This is one of those daily practices you never outgrow. You'll be doing it until the day you retire. On the way to Santiago, this is the walk.

2. Delegation

The second essential practice is delegation. Many leaders delegate poorly—either micromanaging every detail or completely abdicating responsibility. Effective delegation sits in the middle. It's the art of setting clear outcomes while granting your team autonomy over the process.

Delegation done right isn't just about getting work off your plate. It's a development tool. It requires clarity about what success looks like, what resources are available, and what constraints exist. Then it requires trust—to step back and let the person learn through doing. Yes, they may stumble. But if you stay close enough to support without taking over, you're helping them grow their capacity.

When you delegate well, you're not just increasing productivity—you're multiplying capability. You're saying, "I believe you can do more than you think." That's how leadership scales.

3. **Defining Success**

The third practice is setting clear expectations. This one often gets overlooked because leaders assume their teams know what good looks like. But unless you've defined it, tested it, and revisited it, chances are your version of success and theirs aren't perfectly aligned.

Great leaders make success visible. They translate abstract goals into concrete behaviors and measurable outcomes. They make expectations explicit, and they revisit them often—especially when things change. And most importantly, they connect those expectations to the larger mission. They answer the question: Why does this matter?

Done consistently, this practice creates clarity, reduces rework, and builds alignment. But more than that, it gives your people something to aim for—a clear picture of what excellence looks like in their role.

HOLDING IT ALL TOGETHER

And underneath all of this—the one-to-ones, the delegation, the clarity—it's your consistent, steady presence that holds it together. If you're going to help your team manage stress, you have to be able to manage your own. It's like that moment on the airplane: You put your oxygen mask on first so you can help the people around you.

The same goes for leadership. If you can self-regulate—stay calm, grounded, emotionally available—then you can do that for others. And in times like these, that might be the most important skill you bring to the table. It's also what makes you available to really connect. Because so much of what sustains you in the daily walk isn't just discipline or focus. It's the relationships.

THE JOY IS IN THE RELATIONSHIPS

For a long time, I was focused on achievement and execution. I thought leadership was about driving outcomes—about getting the job done. But somewhere along the way, something shifted. I started to see the value of connection—not as a soft skill but as a real source of energy, trust, and resilience. I realized that people don't need you to fix their lives—they just need to know you care. That you're genuinely interested in who they are.

> *People don't need you to fix their lives—they just need to know you care. That you're genuinely interested in who they are.*

At first, it was something I had to practice. I had to remind myself to slow down, to ask questions, to listen with actual curiosity. But over time—months, not days—it stopped feeling like a stretch. It became something I wanted to do. I started noticing just how interesting people are. How much they care. How many good ideas they bring to the table when you create the space for them to show up. And the more I leaned into that, the more it became natural.

Today, I'd say I do this well. But I had to grow into it. I had to realize that connection is part of the work. It's not extra. It's the walk. This, to me, is one of the deepest sources of joy in leadership—not the metrics or the milestones but the relationships. It's about showing up with presence and interest, over and over again, until people start to believe you mean it. That's what creates trust. And trust is what makes the hard parts of leadership worth it.

Reaching this point in my journey has brought me joy—something I've been on a personal journey to rediscover since I was eleven or twelve years old.

When I was ten, baseball was everything to me. I was good at it—really good. Then, around eleven or twelve, my eyesight started to go. I couldn't see the ball anymore. And just like that, I couldn't hit. That season crushed me. The following year, my dad—trying to help—said, "If no one else picks you, I'll put you on a team." He meant well, but I heard it as rejection. I stopped playing. The passion was gone, like something had been ripped out of me.

I picked up swimming after that. I was good at it too—competitive, successful—but it wasn't the same. I swam for the medals, not the joy. And that set a pattern. I had leadership roles, I launched start-ups, and I did meaningful work—but it was always about performance, not passion. I didn't feel that deep connection again until I became a Vistage Chair. That's when the spark came back. The joy. The sense of doing work that mattered and mattered to me.

If you don't love what you're doing—or can't find something in it to love—it's going to be a hard day. And leadership is already hard enough.

There's a phrase I heard once—wish I could remember where—but it stuck with me: the hero in victory and the hero in defeat. We tend to think of ourselves as heroic only when things are going well—when we're crushing our goals, leading the charge, getting results. But the real test is who we are when we're struggling. When we take a step backward. When we fall behind.

It doesn't mean we're not heroic. It means we're on a real journey.

Trying to walk five hundred miles to Santiago, grow a company, develop people, or become a better leader is heroic work. But sometimes the hero's path includes a little retreat. A regrouping. A recentering. As James Clear says in *Atomic Habits*, "it's okay to have a cheat day—just not two in a row."[45]

The work is to keep going. To keep walking. That's the heroism that matters.

---

45 Clear, *Atomic Habits: An Easy & Proven Way to Build Good Habits & Break Bad Ones.*

REFLECTION QUESTIONS/EXERCISES

1. What is one leadership habit or routine you could begin practicing daily?

2. In what part of your leadership do you need to be more deliberate and less reactive?

3. How consistently are you showing up for one-to-ones, and what needs to shift?

4. Who on your team is actively growing—and how are you supporting that growth?

5. What's giving you joy in your leadership right now? Where might you need to reconnect to joy?

In the next chapter, we'll shift from the rhythm of daily practice to something deeper: the inner current that gives that practice meaning. We'll explore what it means to lead in a world where nothing is perfect, permanent, or complete—and why embracing that truth is the beginning of soulful leadership.

CHAPTER 7

SOULFUL LEADERSHIP— LEADING FROM THE INSIDE OUT

*One does not become enlightened by imagining figures
of light, but by making the darkness conscious.*

—CARL JUNG

There's a tension at the heart of every leader's journey—between the greatness we sense we're capable of and the safety we've learned to cling to. It's human nature.

We want to make bold moves—without risking exposure. We want to create meaning—only on familiar terms. We want to lead transformationally—from a place that doesn't feel too dangerous.

As leadership expert Bob Anderson puts it, "We all want to be great, but from a safe place." But here's the truth: We can't do great things from a safe place. It's simply not possible.

That was a hard-won realization for me. For much of my career, I thought I could lead from within the boundaries of what felt comfortable—manage the risk, control the narrative, stay in the lane.

Safe or Purposeful Leadership?

Balancing the tension between staying safe and realizing your vision

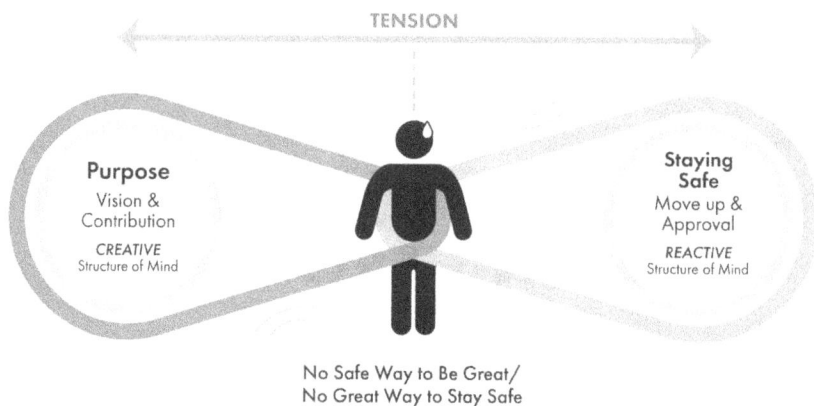

TENSION

Purpose	Staying Safe
Vision & Contribution	Move up & Approval
CREATIVE Structure of Mind	*REACTIVE* Structure of Mind

No Safe Way to Be Great/
No Great Way to Stay Safe

But real leadership doesn't live there. It lives at the edge. The edge of what we know. The edge of what we've done before. The edge of who we've allowed ourselves to become.

That's why this chapter is titled "Soulful Leadership." And yes, I know that word—*soulful*—might make some readers squirm in their seats. I felt it myself, at first. I even considered backing away from it, softening the language. But every time I tried to reframe it—*transformational leadership, mastering leadership*—I kept coming back to the same idea: soul. Because soulful leadership is what I stand for.

Soulful leadership isn't about sentimentality. It's about substance. It's about depth. And it's about reclaiming something essential that too many leaders leave out of the conversation: our humanity.

I remember sitting in my first certification with Bob Anderson over twenty years ago, early in my journey with the Leadership Circle. At one point, Bob started talking about creativity—not as a skill or a style but as a spiritual act. He said that to create is to express the Divine. That landed hard for me. In that moment, I knew I was in the right place.

I believed him.

I still do.

Creativity, at its best, is our divinity in motion. And when we are creating what matters most to us through our leadership—when we are designing, deciding, building, holding space, and choosing again and again to lead with intention—then we are bringing that divinity forward. That's not abstract to me. That's real. That's the work.

But somewhere along the way, many of us learn to constrain that divine force—to narrow the channel, to play it safe. It's as if our life energy is water moving through a hose, and leadership becomes about managing the pressure, twisting the valve, keeping the flow just below the threshold of discomfort.

That's what the reactive identity does. It says, *Stay in control. Don't show too much. Don't risk too much. Don't lose face.*

We close down. We protect. And in doing so, we often lose the very vitality that made us leaders in the first place.

What if leadership could be different?

What if we didn't constrain the flow but expanded our capacity to hold it?

What if leading didn't mean shrinking ourselves but becoming more fully ourselves?

These are the questions that soulful leadership asks. And they're not theoretical. They're deeply practical. Because every time I sit with a CEO who's burning out, second-guessing themselves, or unable to connect with their team, it's not because they lack skill. It's because something essential inside them has been cut off. Something alive, something powerful, something that knows how to lead with clarity and compassion but has been wrapped in layers of fear, armor, and expectations.

Soulful leadership is about reclaiming that missing element. It's about remembering that leadership is not just what we do—it's who we are while we're doing it. It's how we show up. It's what we bring into the room that can't be captured on a spreadsheet.

It's also deeply integrated. The farther I've gone on this journey, the more I've come to see that real leadership isn't built on any one quality—it's what happens when the right forces combine:

- *Physical capacity* gives us the grounded strength to carry the weight of leadership.

- *Spiritual growth* provides the clarity of purpose and deeper meaning that sustains us.

- Together, they produce *authentic presence*—the embodied way we bring all of that into the room.

It's not a model or a checklist. It's a living equation—active, dynamic, moment by moment. When those elements align, something shifts. You don't have to perform leadership. You become it. Not because you're trying harder but because you're more whole. In a sense, you're sculpting leadership from the inside out and the ground up—shaping who you are as much as what you do.

In this chapter, we'll explore how to cultivate that integration—not by adding more to your plate but by reconnecting with what's already inside you. We'll look at how soulful leadership emerges through clarity of values, the practice of intuition, and the courage to be authentic even when it's hard. And we'll ask, together, What kind of leader are you becoming—not just in what you do but in who you are?

LEADING WITH YOUR WHOLE SELF

I didn't just come to think about this integration on the Camino—I lived it. Those five hundred miles showed me that leadership isn't just about the distance you cover. It's leadership as lived embodiment, not just learned technique—a Camino not only of miles but of muscle, meaning, and moment-to-moment mindfulness. Every day demanded something from me—physically, spiritually, and emotionally. And in that daily rhythm, I began to show up differently. Not just walking the miles but walking them fully—in body, in spirit, in presence.

When you do that long enough, something shifts. You start to carry yourself differently. You move from the surface of things to the center. You begin, in a very real sense, to lead as a vessel of integrity.

That's what I want for every leader I coach. Not just more effectiveness. More embodiment. More wisdom. More wakefulness. And the truth is, the tools we use—whether it's the Leadership Circle Profile or a Vistage peer group—are most powerful when they support that inner alignment. Because great leadership isn't just performance. It's alchemy.

And if that language feels a little mythic, good. It should. There's a reason Joseph Campbell, David Whyte, and Robert Kegan are all in conversation with each other in my mind. There's a reason we talk about crucibles, pilgrimages, awakenings. There are no new truths—just new metaphors. And soulful leadership, at its heart, is a return to something ancient: the work of becoming fully human.

THE INNER WORK OF OUTER IMPACT: AUTHENTICITY, PURPOSE, AND VALUES IN ACTION

If authentic presence is what flows from the integration of physical capacity and spiritual depth, then authenticity itself is where most leaders begin to feel the strain. Because being authentic isn't about being yourself—it's about being your *whole* self, on purpose, with rigor. Authenticity is the disciplined practice of aligning who you are with how you lead; authentic presence is the experience others have when that alignment is lived in real time. Authenticity is the inner work—ongoing and often uncomfortable. Authentic presence is what radiates outward when that work is being done.

But before you can lead with authenticity, you need to know what's true for you. That's why I often bring leaders back to values. And not in the corporate, laminated-on-the-wall sense. I mean real, clarified, gut-level, soul-level values—the ones that move you, guide you, and ground you when the stakes are high.

The best tool I've found to help CEOs accomplish this is one we've already talked about: going "three questions deep." I've used it with executives; I've used it in peer groups; and one of the most memorable times I used it was with a team of supervisors at a plumbing company.

The owner had called me in, frustrated that nobody could agree on what *good* looked like in the role. So, I sat down with the team and said, "Let's define it—together." We spent a full day digging in. We used that same questioning approach to get past the obvious and into the real:

If you're a high performer in this role, what do you care about?
Why?
And what does that look like in action?

We talked values. We talked behavior. We talked about the job from the inside out. And by the end of the day, they had written their own shared definition of excellence—one they actually believed in because it came from them.

Here's the secret to what made it work: We removed rank. Everyone's voice mattered equally. Nobody dominated. And I learned that when people are trusted to name what excellence looks like in their world, they rise to it. They show up differently. Not because they've been told to—but because they've been seen. And once people are seen, they begin to care in a different way. It's not just about values on paper—it's about meaning in motion.

When people understand how their role contributes to something greater—whether it's putting a man on the moon or putting dinner on the table—they care more, they give more, and, as a result, they grow more. That's what purpose looks like when it's lived.

Soulful leadership creates space for real ownership. It says: You matter. Your perspective matters. And your growth matters too. And when it's done right, it's not just about culture. It's about transformation.

I'm not saying this kind of leadership is easy. Authenticity is risky. It means showing up without the usual armor. And that scares most of us. We fear being vulnerable. We fear not having the answer. We fear losing approval. And in a business world that often rewards image over integrity, those fears make sense.

When I coach leaders through the Leadership Circle Profile, we often discover that the very things they say they value—honesty, accountability, presence—are also the things they've learned to withhold to stay safe. They tell me, "I value directness, but I don't want to ruffle feathers." Or, "I value transparency, but I don't want to look weak."

This is where soulful leadership starts to take shape—in those moment-to-moment decisions to stop hiding and playing small and risk being seen. It's uncomfortable, but it's also freeing. Because when you stop managing impressions, you start building real trust. And that trust—that willingness to be seen and to see others—clears space for something deeper to emerge: the beginning of wisdom.

CULTIVATING WISDOM

Wisdom in leadership doesn't come from having all the answers. It comes from being awake—attuned to what matters and grounded enough to act on it. That word—*awake*—is the one I keep coming back to. In my experience, the wisest leaders aren't always the smartest or the most strategic; they're the ones who are the most present. The people who've learned how to quiet the noise, slow down the reaction, and notice what has energy.

That's the phrase I use in my coaching: *What has energy?*

Not, *What's the right answer?*

Not, *What should you do?*

Then have the courage to follow the energy.

What's drawing your attention? What stirs something in you? What pulls you forward, even if you don't yet understand why? That's the beginning of intuition—less about having answers, more about sensing orientation. Less about certainty, more about movement.

I've learned to trust those signals in my own life—not just the ones from my head but the ones that show up in my body. A tightening in my chest. A spark behind my eyes. A heaviness in my gut. Those are cues, not conclusions. They're invitations to pay attention. That's wisdom, too—not the final word, but the first spark.

Over time, that shift in attention changed how I understood leadership. I used to think it was about solving problems. Now I think it's about *sensing into them.* This is where the science catches up with the soul.

Psychiatrist and former Oxford literary scholar Iain McGilchrist's work on the brain hemispheres[46] has helped me understand that what we often describe as *intuition* isn't vague or soft. It's whole-brain integration. The left hemisphere gives us focus, detail, and analysis. The right gives us context, pattern, and meaning. When we're operating in a reactive mindset, we're often stuck in the left hemisphere—calculating,

---

46 Iain McGilchrist, *The Master and His Emissary: The Divided Brain and the Making of the Western World* (New Haven: Yale University Press, 2009).

controlling, narrowing the field. But when we move into a creative mindset, the hemispheres begin to work together. And something opens up.

That's more than a poetic idea—it's backed by neuroscience. Research by Sara Lazar and others into long-term mindfulness practices, such as meditation, has proven that they increase the neural connectivity between the hemispheres.[47]

The impact goes far beyond stress relief. These practices help us become more *adaptive*, more *integrated*, and more capable of meeting complexity with clarity. And that's the foundation of wise leadership: not leaning on one mode but drawing from many. Thinking and feeling. Data and instinct. Presence and action.

This kind of integration—of the inner and outer games, left and right brains, spiritual depth and strategic execution—is what I think of as integral leadership. It's the synthesis we've been building toward all along: a metaframework that holds the complexity, dynamism, and humanity of real leadership. It doesn't isolate one dimension or prioritize one at the expense of the rest—it brings them all together into a full-bodied, full-hearted way of being in the work.

This approach to leadership draws inspiration from frameworks such as Ken Wilber's Integral Theory,[48] which maps development across multiple dimensions of reality—inner and outer, individual and collective. Leadership at its highest level brings together personal growth, practical skill, cultural awareness, and systemic insight into a living, evolving presence.

I've come to believe that when a leader is fully awake—when their inner and outer games are aligned, when their body and brain are

---

47   Sara Lazar et al., "Meditation Experience Is Associated with Increased Cortical Thickness," *NeuroReport* 16, no. 17 (2005): 1893–1897.

48   Ken Wilber, *A Theory of Everything: An Integral Vision for Business, Politics, Science, and Spirituality.*

communicating, when their awareness is tuned to what matters—they don't just make better decisions. They *are* the decision. They move the room by how they enter it. They listen in a way that makes other people think more clearly. They notice things others miss because they're paying attention.

And that's the thread that runs through all of this. Soulful leadership isn't about performing wisdom. It's about practicing it. Living it. Day by day, choice by choice, moment by moment.

Joseph Campbell once said, "The way to find out about your happiness is to keep your mind on those moments when you feel most happy … not ecstatic, not thrilled, but deeply happy."[49] I would say the same is true for leadership. Pay attention to when you feel most alive, most grounded, most aligned. That's the place to lead from. That's the place where wisdom lives.

THE CRUCIBLE OF TRANSFORMATION

However, as Campbell reminds us, awakening is just one part of the journey. The path to transformation always runs through trial. You don't just know your values—you test them. You live them.

It's not easy.

The Leadership Circle calls this "courageous authenticity"—the willingness to take tough stands, speak undiscussable truths, and navigate difficult relational terrain without shutting down or selling out. It's one of the hardest capacities to develop because it forces you to confront your own contradictions. To ask: *Do I actually walk my talk? Or do I make exceptions for people who produce results?*

---

49 "Joseph Campbell Quotable Quotes," Goodreads, accessed July 11, 2025, https://www.goodreads.com/quotes/444342-the-way-to-find-out-about-happiness-is-to-keep.

I've coached more than a few CEOs who let star performers get away with behavior that went against everything they said they believed in. And every time they did, it sent a clear message to the rest of the team: *We don't actually live our values—we rent them when it's convenient.*

That's not leadership. That's compromise disguised as pragmatism.

Real authenticity demands more. It asks you to see the gap between who you say you are and how you actually lead—and to close it.

And that kind of growth doesn't happen in isolation.

Years ago, I read Robert Kegan's description of what real developmental growth requires. He talked about a "crucible experience"—something that applies just enough pressure to spark change without overwhelming a person.[50] Too much safety and nothing shifts. Too much stress and the system collapses. But in the right container—with the right balance of challenge and support—real transformation becomes possible. That's what a great peer group does.

I've described Vistage peer groups as crucibles before—but this is where that metaphor truly comes to life. These groups create a space where you can bring your whole self—wisdom, doubt, ambition, edge—and be fully held. Feedback isn't decorative; it's expected. Accountability isn't a threat; it's a gift. You're not just pushed to perform—you're called to grow.

I've seen it over and over again in my own work. A leader walks into their first Vistage meeting still wearing the armor of their title. They want to impress. They want to be seen as capable. But over time—through the rhythm of real conversation, the trust of shared experience, the honesty of hard feedback—they begin to shed that

---

50   Robert Kegan, as cited in Amelia Broughton, "Successful People All Have This Experience in Common," *Thoughtleader School*, August 2023.

armor. They start to tell the truth. They stop needing to be the smartest person in the room. And something opens up. That's the moment I wait for. Because that's when the real work begins.

This kind of container—a crucible of growth—can't be faked or forced. It requires intention. It requires design. But mostly, it requires commitment: the willingness to keep showing up, again and again, not to prove yourself but to grow yourself. And that's the heart of the leadership journey.

Soulful leadership doesn't emerge fully formed. It's forged. In reflection. In community. In discomfort. And in the daily discipline of staying open to what you're becoming. Because while the crucible may be where something breaks open, consistency is what tempers the metal. The leaders who endure and evolve aren't chasing intensity. They're returning to the walk, day after day. *Consistency* versus *intensity* is a key distinction to learn, value, and develop.

In other words, the change we're after comes from walking fifteen to twenty miles every day on the Camino, through heat, doubt, and pain. The rhythm becomes the revelation. Not the peak but the practice.

That's how leadership works. Breakthroughs are powerful, but they don't sustain you. What does is showing up daily. The quiet follow-through. The steady commitment to what matters most. Soulful leadership doesn't spike—it endures. It isn't driven by adrenaline but by attention. And over time, that kind of attention—faithful, focused, and steady—becomes something more. It becomes a transformation.

> *What emerges isn't just a better version of what was. It's something entirely new.*

We touched on the metaphor of alchemy earlier. This is where it comes full circle. Because if soulful leadership is a kind of transformation, then maybe what we're really practicing is alchemy. The alchemist doesn't just add ingredients—they hold them in fire. They work with time, with pressure, with devotion. And what emerges isn't just a better version of what was. It's something entirely new.

That's what we do when we coach. When we lead. When we hold others through their crucibles. We become, in a quiet way, leadership alchemists—blending ambition with alignment, strategy with soul, performance with presence. Not with magic. With attention.

BECOMING THE LEGACY

At some point in every leader's journey, the question shifts from *What am I building?* to *What am I leaving behind?*

It's not just about numbers or outcomes. It's about the impact. How did people feel in your presence? What did they believe was possible because of you? What values did you reinforce, simply by how you led? That's the beginning of legacy—not as something that comes later but as something you're shaping every day. In that sense, soulful leadership is legacy in motion.

One of the most intentional leaders I've worked with was Matt Dean, the founder of a company called Markon. When I first asked him what he ultimately wanted from the business, he didn't lead with metrics or financial targets. He said, "I want to create Markon millionaires."

And he meant it.

Over the years, he gave equity to key employees who demonstrated real commitment to the mission. He held them to a high standard—but he modeled it first. He poured himself into every one-to-one, every Vistage meeting, every strategic conversation about culture. And when he eventually sold the company, he had done exactly what he had set out to do: He had created fourteen Markon millionaires—not including himself.

Matt didn't just create wealth—he created a culture in which growth was expected, rewarded, and deeply shared. That's legacy by design. But legacy isn't always about wealth or scale. Sometimes, it's about modeling something people didn't believe was possible. Sometimes, it's about the ripple effects of integrity—what people do after watching how you handled something hard.

That's the legacy of soulful leadership: a presence that lasts. It lives on in how others carry forward what you stood for—in the clarity, courage, or calm they found through your example. This kind of leadership doesn't need to be loud to leave a mark. It stays because it was real.

The work is simple, but not easy: Show up with enough depth and attention that your presence continues to shape the room, even after you've left it. Become the kind of leader who makes others braver by the way you carry yourself.

Leadership is temporary. Legacy isn't.

And here's the paradox: The more present you are in this moment, the more lasting your impact becomes. Soulful leadership isn't a role, a title, or a style. It's a way of being.

Over time, it becomes less something you do and more who you are. It shows up in your presence, your pace, your posture, your patterns. It's not about being flawless. It's about being aligned—inside and out—with what matters most. People feel that. They trust it. And they grow because of it.

That's the real legacy—not just your results but your ripple.

Because in the end, soulful leadership isn't a technique. It's a life.

REFLECTION QUESTIONS/EXERCISES

1. Where in your leadership are you showing up most fully right now—in body, in presence, or in purpose?

2. What part of your leadership might still be driven by safety over soul?

3. What do you want people to say about you when you're no longer in the room?

4. What kind of crucible are you holding for the people you lead?

5. What legacy are you becoming—right now, in the way you lead today?

In the next chapter, we'll explore what it means to lead with a different kind of attention—not as a tactic but as a practice of perception—when we explore my third Camino revelation: Travel with soft eyes.

CHAPTER 8

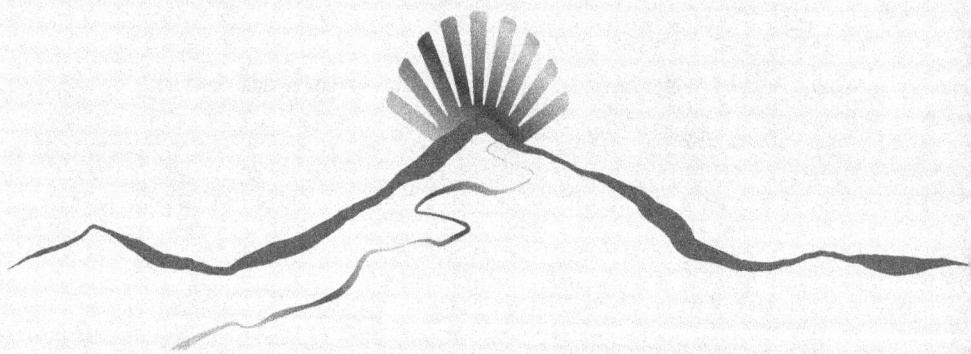

TRAVEL WITH SOFT EYES

> *The leader of the past knew how to tell,*
> *the leader of the future will know how to ask.*

—PETER DRUCKER

The Camino is marked—just enough to keep a pilgrim moving forward but never so clearly that you can stop paying attention. There are yellow arrows and drawings of scallop shells posted to guide the way, painted on stone walls, etched into signposts, laid into cobblestone streets. But they're not always obvious. You have to stay alert.

And yet—there I was, walking through one of those ancient medieval towns, and I came to an intersection with no clear signage. And even though I'd never walked the Camino before, had no reference point, no confirmation—I was absolutely certain I needed to turn left.

So I did.

And walked two miles on aching knees in the wrong direction.

I did that more than once.

One time, a local villager spotted me and shouted, "Peregrino! It's this way!" And it landed like a little smack from the universe:

Dude. Stop making it up. You have no idea what you're talking about.

That moment broke something open. I realized how tightly I'd been gripping the need to know, to be right, to stay in control. I wasn't missing the signs because they weren't there. I was missing them because I wasn't really seeing.

That's when the shift happened—my Camino revelation: Travel with soft eyes.

To travel with soft eyes is a perceptual shift. It's a way of walking, listening, and leading that trades certainty for presence. It invites you to stay open to what's unfolding in front of you instead of charging ahead with the plan you made two miles ago.

It also gets to the heart of something Robert Kegan writes in *Immunity to Change*:

"If you're leading anything at any level, you're driving some kind of plan or agenda—but some kind of plan or agenda is also driving you."[51]

That's the invisible terrain most leaders are walking. We're being run—often unknowingly—by the same success strategies we've been talking about throughout this book. Built early, reinforced often, they become our default settings:

Move fast.

Stay in control.

Avoid risk.

Prove your value.

But these old strategies don't always serve the journey we're actually on. In fact, they often get in the way—locking us into reactive patterns that keep us from seeing the arrow carved into the post or the shell among the cobblestones that marks the way forward. Until we can name what's driving us, we can't choose a different path.

---

51   Robert Kegan and Lisa Laskow Lahey, *The Immunity to Change* (Harvard Business Review Press, 2009).

So in this chapter, we're going to focus on what it means to travel with soft eyes.

STRAIN LESS, SEE MORE

The phrase *soft eyes* comes from martial arts. It refers to a relaxed, unfocused gaze that lets you take in the whole field—not just your opponent. In the early days of my pilgrimage, it felt like the Camino itself was my opponent. I was out to conquer it. I'd catch myself scanning the trail ahead, hyperfocused, trying to spot the next marker, the next town, the next stretch of road. But when I softened my gaze—literally—I saw more. The landscape opened up. So did my awareness. I wasn't just moving through the terrain—I was part of it.

And I realized: The more I relaxed my focus, the more present I became. The less I strained to see, the more clearly I could perceive. That was the shift. I had adopted a pilgrim mindset—not trying to conquer the path but to walk with it. To stay open to whatever was unfolding, without forcing a destination.

Leadership calls for that same sort of mindset.

Soft eyes are a way of seeing—and a way of being. They represent a shift in perception: from a narrow focus to expanded awareness, from striving to openness. This isn't about being deliberately vague or checked out. It's about easing our grip—on outcomes, on stories, on the need for certainty—and allowing a fuller view to emerge.

Soft eyes still notice the details, but they don't cling to them. They don't rush to make meaning. They wait. They sense. They include.

Ironically, it was only when I started leading with soft eyes that I realized this wasn't just about what I was seeing. It was about how I was listening.

Over time, one of the most profound shifts in my leadership—and especially in my coaching—has been in how I listen. I don't mean listening harder or asking better questions. I mean letting go of the need to listen with a plan. I come in with no agenda, no angle, no impulse to solve.

I no longer approach a conversation with the goal of delivering a breakthrough or steering it toward insight. That kind of listening is still about control. It may look skillful on the surface, but underneath it's reactive. It's about making something happen instead of allowing the best solution to unfold.

What I do now is different. I listen with all the wisdom centers— my Curious Mind, my Open Heart, and my Instinctual Gut. I pay attention not just to the words but to the tone, the energy, the silences, the facial expressions, the shifts in posture. I stay fully present to the person, not to my idea of what I think they need.

That shift has freed me from the need to be seen as smart or competent. That's not what's driving me anymore. And in letting go of that old success strategy—the one that says I have to have the answer—I've made space for something much deeper: presence, curiosity, and the instinct to follow what's unfolding rather than force what's next.

This is what soft eyes feel like in practice. Not just a way of seeing but a way of receiving. And in leadership, that posture makes all the difference.

LEADING WITH SOFT EYES

Soft eyes might sound like a personal practice, but they're essential in leadership—especially in the fast-moving, uncertain environments leaders face today. The days of linear problems and simple solutions are over. Most leaders are operating in dynamic systems, where cause and effect aren't clear, perspectives often collide, and clarity takes time to emerge.

In that kind of terrain, a narrow focus can do more harm than good. It limits perspective, adds pressure, and pushes people toward premature decisions. Soft eyes offer something else. They widen your field of view. They help you stay grounded in complexity, attuned to what's unfolding. With soft eyes, you can sense patterns, catch early signals, and stay with ambiguity a little longer. You can track what's happening beneath the surface while staying present to what's in front of you.

In practice, this way of seeing strengthens some of the most important capacities a leader can bring to complexity.

- **Adaptive Capacity**

Soft eyes allow you to respond rather than react. You stay in the conversation long enough to notice what's really going on—patterns, dynamics, emotional undercurrents—without becoming overwhelmed or shutting down.

- **Systemic Awareness**

You see more than isolated problems. You begin to see the whole system—the relationships between people, timing, structure, and culture—and how those elements interact.

- **Presence and Empathy**

When your eyes are soft, your presence is too. People feel it. They're more willing to engage when they sense openness, calm, and curiosity.

- **Spiritual and Emotional Intelligence**

Soft eyes reflect an internal stillness and external openness. They don't rush to judge or fix. They create space for something deeper to emerge—what we might call wisdom.

That's why soft eyes aren't just helpful—they reflect something more fundamental. They mark a shift in how a leader sees, thinks, and operates. No wonder the most influential frameworks in leadership development all point to this same evolution.

The Leadership Circle calls it the movement from reactive to creative leadership. Soft eyes support that transition by loosening our grip on control, perfection, or pleasing, and grounding us instead in purpose, integrity, and systems thinking. Heifetz's Adaptive Leadership model reinforces the point. Adaptive challenges can't be solved with expertise alone—they require presence, reflection, and the ability to see the bigger picture without rushing to action. That kind of leadership depends on soft perception and steady attention.

Kegan's adult development theory adds another layer. In his framework, soft eyes reflect later-stage leadership maturity—a sign that we've moved beyond being shaped by external expectations and into a deeper capacity to hold paradox, embrace complexity, and lead with humility.

These aren't just the insights of leadership science—they echo the larger human questions we've wrestled with forever. What does it mean to grow? To see clearly? To lead wisely? These frameworks give shape to a transformation that is as ancient as it is urgent.

For the leadership journeyman, soft eyes mark a threshold. A shift away from old strategies designed to keep us safe and toward a more conscious, present way of leading. A movement from habit to choice. From survival to service.

Because a Camino isn't about collecting new tools; it's about transformation. It's about becoming someone new. And when that begins to happen—when insights, frameworks, and lived experiences start to converge—you lead differently. You stop forcing clarity and start allowing it. You stay open. You stay awake. And leadership becomes what it was always meant to be: a living conversation with the complexity around you.

THE SUBTLE PULL OF BIAS

Soft eyes don't just help us see the world more clearly. They help us see our own minds at work. That's often where the real work begins—because no matter how experienced we are, every leader carries unconscious distortions. With the amount of data and complexity we face every day, our minds are constantly deleting, distorting, and generalizing. It's how we cope. We can't possibly take it all in.

But when those mental shortcuts become habitual—and we stop noticing them—they start to lead us off course. This is where bias enters the picture. Not as a flaw to fix but as a natural byproduct of the systems we've built to survive.

As leaders, we all carry biases—assumptions, preferences, stories we tell ourselves that shape what we notice and how we respond. Most of the time, they're invisible. That's what makes them powerful.

The one I see most often in my work is confirmation bias: the tendency to seek out data that supports what we already believe and to filter out what doesn't. It's incredibly common—and incredibly human. But it keeps us in a loop. We're no longer learning. We're reinforcing.

There's also overconfidence bias—the sense that because we've seen something before, we understand it fully. Or attribution bias, when we claim success but externalize failure. And then there's groupthink—when the desire for harmony or efficiency keeps a leadership team from voicing disagreement. It often shows up in executive rooms where everyone is "aligned," but nobody's telling the truth.

Biases such as these aren't just mental shortcuts. They're signs that something in our reactive system is still running the show. Soft eyes give us another option. They help us pause, open our awareness, and ask the following questions:

What story might I be clinging to here?

What am I not seeing?

The leadership journeyman's path is one of progressive self-awareness. It's a walk through unfamiliar terrain—both out in the world and inside ourselves. And bias is like a hidden rut in the road. If we're not watching for it, we fall into it—again and again. The inner work we need to do is clear:

- Move from unconscious bias to conscious noticing to deliberate repatterning.

- Develop metacognition—the ability to think about how you think.

- Practice humility, curiosity, and perspective-taking as daily disciplines, not just occasional efforts.

Because if we don't surface and soften our biases, they don't just limit our own growth. They ripple out into every conversation, every decision, every culture we try to shape. When bias stays unconscious, it shows up everywhere:

- Leaders stay stuck in reactive mindsets.

- They confuse certainty with clarity.

- They repeat poor decisions without learning.

- They struggle to adapt when complexity demands more from them.

Different frameworks define bias in different ways—but they're all getting at the same thing: Unconscious patterns shape our leadership unless we do the work to bring them into the light. In the Leadership Circle, bias often shows up through reactive tendencies—controlling, protecting, or complying—before we even realize it. In *Immunity to Change*, Kegan and Lahey show how unseen biases can mask the deeper commitments that block our growth. The adult development theory reminds us that moving from the socialized mind to the self-authoring mind requires disrupting old patterns of seeing. Even in Vistage groups, some of the most powerful breakthroughs happen when trusted peers help surface the assumptions we can't yet see in ourselves.

This is why the journey matters. Seeing bias clearly isn't a side-note to leadership. It's the beginning of choosing a different way. And like any shift in awareness, it starts small. It starts with the daily noticing.

One of the simplest and most effective ways I advise my clients to work with bias is to keep a bias journal. At the end of the day, simply ask yourself: *Where did I make assumptions today? What story was I convinced of, and how might I have missed something?* Over time, this kind of gentle inquiry builds real self-awareness.

I also encourage leaders to invite in the contrarian—the person who sees things differently from them. Not to debate them but to listen longer. That perspective often reveals where our own filters are still operating, or where groupthink might be quietly narrowing the field of view.

And perhaps most importantly, I advise them to slow the loop. When urgency or the pressure to be right shows up, it's worth pausing and asking yourself, *What's really driving this reaction?* Bias thrives on speed. Wisdom lives in the pause.

Because in the end, soft eyes aren't just about how we see the world. They're about how we see ourselves. When we can meet our own distortions with curiosity instead of judgment, we create the possibility for real growth. Not by forcing it. Not by fixing ourselves. But by staying awake, even when it would be easier to slip back into certainty. That's the quiet discipline of the leadership journeyman: learning to walk a little lighter, a little more aware, every day.

SOFT EYES AND THE LISTENING BODY

Real wisdom in leadership doesn't come from having all the answers. It comes from creating the conditions in which real conversations can happen. Leadership isn't just about solving problems—it's about listening with enough presence to be changed by what you hear and see. Soft eyes and active listening form a kind of posture—a way of staying open, curious, and attentive to what's unfolding, without trying to control it.

> *Soft eyes and active listening form a kind of posture—a way of staying open, curious, and attentive to what's unfolding, without trying to control it.*

Active listening is more than hearing words. It's taking in the full shape of communication—the meaning, the emotion, the context. I've experienced personally how soft eyes deepen that listening. They help you receive what's being shared without tension, judgment, or the need to respond right away.

Together, soft eyes and active listening create what I call the *listening body* of a leader, engaging all three wisdom centers: the mind, the heart, and the gut.

The Curious Mind stays alert. The Open Heart stays open. And the Instinctual Gut stays attuned. It's a full-bodied way of leading. And when it's practiced, something shifts: People feel seen, not evaluated. Heard, not managed. Met, not maneuvered.

One of the clearest examples I've seen of soft eyes and active listening in leadership came from one of my Vistage members. During the unrest that followed the murder of George Floyd, this CEO—who leads a very diverse workforce—could feel the tension rising inside her company.

There was fear. There was anger. There was uncertainty about how to even begin to talk about what was happening. And she understood intuitively that if she didn't create space for the conversation, it would find a voice of its own—and not necessarily in ways that would strengthen the culture she had worked so hard to build. So she decided to take it on.

She crafted an email to her entire organization, setting clear but compassionate guidelines for how they could engage. She invited people to share how they were being affected—emotionally, personally, humanly. She made it safe to express pain and perspective. But she also set strong boundaries: no pontificating, no politicizing, no turning the space into a battleground of opinions. You could share your experience, you could share your feelings, but you couldn't weaponize them.

It was as masterful a piece of leadership as I've ever seen.

Because it wasn't just about controlling the conversation—it was about modeling the kind of presence she wanted others to practice. Soft eyes. Open hearts. An active willingness to listen to experiences that might not be your own without needing to agree or disagree. Simply allowing the space for it to exist.

What emerged was exactly what you might expect: two camps, two different points of view. But there was also something deeper— something that CEO had made possible. A healthy respect. An insistence on real listening. A model of leadership that didn't demand alignment but created connection.

This Vistage member later shared this story with my CEO groups, and it left an impression on all of us. Because it wasn't theory. It was leadership alive and awake in the moment.

Leadership moments such as these show us something essential: that active listening isn't passive. That presence isn't weakness. And that soft eyes aren't about stepping back from challenge—they're about stepping into it differently—with grounded openness and the willingness to stay present long enough for something new to emerge.

When we can hold that kind of presence—when we can stay open even when the path isn't clear—something deeper becomes possible. To lead not by fixing but by sensing. To move not by knowing but by noticing. To stay present long enough for the next step to reveal itself. This is where soft eyes become more than a way of seeing. They become a way of walking.

LEADING WITHOUT A MAP

On the Camino, there were moments when I had to trust that the next marker would show up when I needed it. Leadership often asks the same thing of us: to keep walking without knowing exactly where we're headed. Especially now. We talk about VUCA, but it's the complexity and ambiguity parts that most often trip us up.

Complexity means there are too many moving parts to be reduced to simple cause and effect.

Ambiguity means we don't just lack clarity—we're unsure what things even mean.

In a complex and ambiguous environment, hard eyes fall back on old patterns. They narrow the field. They rush to impose order. They reach for quick answers in a world that no longer rewards them.

Soft eyes do something else. They pause. They create space. They stay open long enough for new possibilities to emerge—possibilities that would stay hidden under a narrower gaze. Don't think of it as passive waiting; think of it as active receptivity. It's about noticing what's unfolding rather than trying to control it.

That's where creativity lives—not under pressure or precision but in space. In uncertainty. In the willingness to sit with what hasn't formed yet. Soft eyes help us see the signals we'd otherwise miss. And when we lead from that place, insight becomes possible. Innovation becomes possible. You can't create from a rigid stance because hard eyes demand resolution too soon. Soft eyes give ambiguity the space it needs to ripen into insight.

> *That's where creativity lives—not under pressure or precision but in space.*

Leaders don't always know what's coming next—and that's the point. The journey isn't about conquering the terrain. It's about becoming the kind of person who can walk it with humility, curiosity, and the awareness to notice small signals before they turn into something larger.

Every major framework we've explored supports this same truth: The leaders who thrive in complexity are the ones who stay open, stay present, and stay willing to learn. In the Leadership Circle, complexity tends to trigger reactive patterns—controlling, protecting, complying—especially when leaders fall back on old success strategies. Soft eyes help shift us to the top of the circle and into our creative competencies: systems thinking, authentic presence, self-awareness, learning to respond instead of react.

In Heifetz's Adaptive Leadership model, technical challenges can be solved with expertise, but adaptive challenges—where both the problem and the solution are unclear—require leaders with soft eyes to observe, interpret, and act without rushing to closure. And in Kegan's adult development theory, soft eyes reflect the evolution into the self-transforming mind—the capacity to hold contradiction and complexity without losing your center.

These aren't just theoretical shifts. They're practical capacities that help leadership work—especially when things are unclear. Soft eyes keep us grounded and responsive in a world that no longer plays by simple rules. Just like on the Camino, leadership asks us to move forward without needing to see the whole path. We don't advance by forcing clarity—we move forward by trusting the next step will emerge when it's time.

This brings me back to the concept of deliberate practice that we explored earlier. The small, steady work of training ourselves to adopt new ways of seeing, thinking, and leading is exactly that kind of practice. It's about returning, again and again, to a different way of being with the world. Less tension. More space. Less rush. More receptivity.

But deliberate practice doesn't always feel like that. It feels uncomfortable because it brings friction. Especially when the stakes rise, soft eyes can feel unnatural—too slow, too uncertain, too exposed. In those moments, old instincts return with force, narrowing our focus when we most need to widen it:

- the urge to act fast

- the pressure to perform

- the need to be right

- the discomfort of ambiguity

- the fear of losing control

Each of these moments offers a choice. We can tighten—or we can soften. We can react—or we can widen our gaze. Here's how soft eyes invite us to meet these moments differently.

• The Urge to Act Fast

Old pattern: You rushed to decide and jumped into action to relieve discomfort.

Soft eyes practice: Pause. Breathe. Widen your view.

Ask yourself: *What's truly urgent here—and what might emerge if I waited just ninety more seconds?*

- **The Pressure to Perform**

Old pattern: You felt the need to know, fix, or prove competence.

Soft eyes practice: Shift from solving to sensing.

Ask yourself: *What's the most important question I could be curious about right now?*

- **The Need to Be Right**

Old pattern: You filtered reality through old assumptions or experiences.

Soft eyes practice: Invite fresh perspectives.

Ask yourself: *What's another way of seeing this?*

- **The Discomfort of Ambiguity**

Old pattern: You grasped for quick answers to soothe uncertainty.

Soft eyes practice: Stay with the not knowing.

Remind yourself: *This fog isn't failure. It's fertile.*

- **The Fear of Losing Control**

Old pattern: You gripped harder, narrowed your field of vision, and defended your identity.

Soft eyes practice: Soften inside first.

Remind yourself: *I don't have to be the answer. I can be the space where the answer emerges.*

These daily practices are small openings that widen the path over time. And sometimes, those small shifts open the door to extraordinary results. Another Vistage member I work with offered a powerful example of this in real time.

This CEO runs a company that specializes in helping organizations drive behavior change through projects such as public health campaigns to reduce smoking. After the 2016 election, when political priorities shifted dramatically, her company was hit hard. Contracts dried up almost overnight.

So, years later, when another wave of political change was on the horizon, this CEO took a different approach. Instead of waiting for the impact to hit, she and her team began intentionally exploring new possibilities. They didn't panic. They didn't lock into one solution. They stayed curious. They asked, "Where else might we be relevant? What emerging spaces could use our skills?"

When funding streams began shifting again, they were ready. They landed the largest contract in their company's history with a state government agency—because they had softened their gaze, stayed open, and prepared without knowing exactly what would emerge.

This story is a brilliant reminder: Leadership isn't about predicting the future. It's about preparing ourselves to meet it—with creativity, adaptability, and trust. It's about walking with soft eyes—especially when we can't yet see the road ahead.

When I think back on my own Camino, what stays with me the most isn't the distance covered or the challenges overcome. It's what I came to value in the walking itself.

Stillness. Presence. Intentional awareness. Gratitude. Wonder.

Before the Camino, I had a bias for action. I was a busyness junkie—constantly moving, solving, doing. I believed that control and certainty were the ways to stay safe and succeed. But the Camino changed that.

I learned that I didn't have to figure everything out. I didn't have to know every turn in advance. I didn't have to control every aspect of the journey. Everything I needed would be there, one step at a time. And that realization didn't make me less effective. It made me more present, more trusting, more whole. I stopped seeing leadership as a performance to master and started seeing it as a walk to be taken—with soft eyes, steady feet, and an open heart.

REFLECTION QUESTIONS/EXERCISES

1. In what parts of your leadership right now are you practicing soft eyes—and what's beginning to shift because of it?

2. Where do you notice yourself falling back into hard eyes—rushing, controlling, narrowing your focus?

3. What would it look like to widen your view instead of narrowing it in the face of uncertainty?

4. What small daily practice could help you meet complexity with more curiosity, more patience, and more presence?

5. What are you starting to trust more deeply—not because you control it but because you are willing to walk with it?

In many ways, learning to lead with soft eyes is the beginning of arriving—not at a final destination but at a different way of being on the journey itself. In the next section of this book, we'll explore what it means to arrive and begin anew—to recognize and celebrate the milestones along our leadership path without mistaking them for the journey's end.

CHAPTER 9

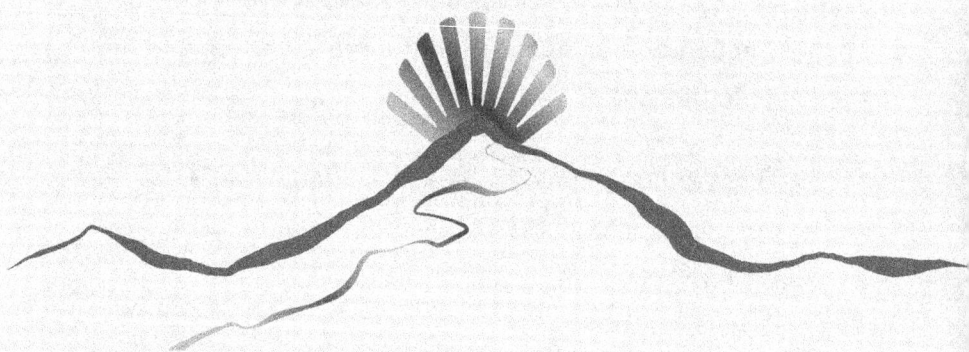

ARRIVAL AT SANTIAGO— CELEBRATING THE MILESTONES

*The end of all our exploring will be to arrive where
we started and know the place for the first time.*

—T. S. ELIOT

When I got to Santiago, my knees were killing me. The backs of them had swollen up so badly that I could barely bend them. I honestly don't think I could have walked much further—I got there just in time.

I had walked the last stretch alone. I remember entering the courtyard of the cathedral—this big, open square filled with people from all over the world, with pilgrims arriving from every direction. I felt my exhaustion give way to this incredible feeling of arrival and celebration. I had done it. And I wasn't alone. I was part of something bigger—this community of people who had each completed something mythological in their own way.

I don't remember if it was that same day or the next, but I stood in line for about forty-five minutes to get my *Compostela*, the official certificate of completion. I showed my pilgrim passport to prove I'd made the journey. Two Australian women were behind me in line—we got into this great conversation about the different routes. They had taken the Portuguese path, and it struck me again that there really are many ways to get to Santiago.

I went to the Pilgrim's Mass. I saw the swinging of the Botafumeiro, this huge incense burner flying across the cathedral. It was extraordinary. Every morning, I got up early and sat in that cathedral—just to sit there. I spent three days doing that. I didn't try to analyze it. I just let the space and the silence have their way with me. I had made it.

But the truth is, all I could think about was the thirty-five days of walking. That's what had changed me. Santiago was beautiful, sacred, full of tradition—but the real transformation happened on the road. I had set out with a goal, but it turned out that the destination wasn't the point. The walking was the point. The rhythm. The grind. The slow unfolding of who I was becoming.

It would take me months to fully understand it, but I knew something in me had shifted. Santiago was a moment of arrival, yes—but not in the way I had expected. I began to see celebration in a new way: not as a burst of emotion at the end but as a quiet honoring of the path that had shaped me. The destination mattered, but only because of the road that led me there.

That's what this chapter is about—celebrating the journey. Not just the peaks but the process. Not just the results but the growth along the way.

MASTERY AND OPTIMIZATION

After weeks of walking the Camino—through pain, exhaustion, and the daily grind of one foot after the other—arriving in Santiago wasn't just a finish line. It was a milestone of a different kind: the quiet celebration of mastery.

But what is mastery, really?

True mastery is paradoxical. It is both a stage and a place and a series of arrivals—and it never fully ends. In leadership, particularly for the leadership journeyman, mastery is a commitment to keep walking, even after apparent summits are reached. You occupy it for a time—a phase, a moment, a place in a larger developmental journey where deep competence and wisdom are actively present.

> *True mastery is paradoxical. It is both a stage and a place and a series of arrivals—and it never fully ends.*

By the time I arrived in Santiago, I had the skills, the knowledge, and the internal steadiness needed to complete the journey. I had become a kind of master pilgrim—not because the path got easier but because I had grown into someone who could meet it with presence and readiness. Mastery, as I experienced it, wasn't about accumulating technique. It was best understood as an evolving relationship with skill, self, and life itself. A profound integration of skill, wisdom, and being.

Each arrival expands the landscape. Each stage gives way to deeper terrain. The place you inhabit grows larger, more integrated, more soulfully resonant. Arrival moments are thresholds, not end points—mastery reveals new mountains beyond the peak you thought was the summit.

Still, mastery alone didn't carry me across Spain. Just as essential was something quieter: optimization.

Optimization, for the leadership journeyman, is not about doing more—it's about doing better, simpler, and truer. It's the art of stripping away noise, refining things to their essence, and aligning action with meaning. It's not a single change but an ongoing, dynamic process that sharpens awareness, refines action, integrates learning, and compounds impact over time.

On the Camino, optimization meant learning how many miles I could walk without blowing out my knees. It meant streamlining my routines—when to wake up, when to rest, what to carry, what to leave behind. It meant conserving energy for the long journey ahead. Not just physical energy but mental and emotional energy too.

Over time, I found a rhythm—clear, repeatable, sustainable. That rhythm wasn't something I figured out on day one. I earned it mile by mile, through feedback, recalibration, and the slow art of iteration.

Leadership works the same way. I've watched CEOs charge forward with endless meetings, bloated agendas, and heroic sprints that leave them depleted. They assume more motion means more progress. But more meetings don't make you a better leader. Busier schedules don't lead to more effective influence. More expertise doesn't necessarily result in deeper wisdom.

Instead, what makes the difference is focus—on the vital few over the trivial many. This is the 80/20 rule in action: 80 percent of your results come from 20 percent of your actions. Optimized leaders learn to identify and concentrate their energy on those few moves that generate the greatest returns.

They simplify systems and habits for clarity and speed. They streamline communication, meetings, and workflows so that complexity doesn't drain the team's capacity. They align the inner game—values, intuition, discernment—with the outer game of strategy and influence. They prioritize energy, not just time. And they treat every project, every challenge, every conversation as a chance to iterate toward mastery—not as a verdict but as feedback.

That's what real optimization looks like. It's what lets leaders move systems, hearts, and results with minimal wasted effort and maximum authenticity. The clients I've worked with who embrace this shift don't just perform better. They begin to lead from a quieter, more grounded place. The clutter drops away. Their leadership becomes cleaner, more elegant, more precise.

They're not striving to do everything. They're learning to do the right things—and to do them with intention. Over time, this way of operating becomes a kind of artistry. The work doesn't vanish—but it stops draining you. You recover faster. You communicate with more impact. You trust your discernment more deeply. And you begin to adopt a leadership style that's no longer driven by pressure but by clarity.

Through experience and reflection, you stop adding weight to your pack. You travel lighter. Wiser. More intentionally. Like the Camino, leadership becomes a matter of rhythm. You walk your miles each day—through fatigue, frustration, and uncertainty—and still pause to acknowledge what the day required of you.

That acknowledgment matters. The leaders who thrive are the ones who mark their progress as they go. They don't wait for the summit. They honor the daily march.

Mastery and optimization, when paired, become less about arriving and more about sustaining. They help leaders grow with their challenges, not against them. And they make it possible to celebrate the road—not just the destination.

THE POWER OF ACKNOWLEDGMENT

For the leadership journeyman—someone beyond a beginner but still forging their way toward mastery—recognition and celebration are not luxuries. They are essential nutrients for motivation, resilience, and identity formation. Without moments of reflection and acknowledgment, even the most committed leader risks falling into three traps: burnout, self-doubt, and stagnation. That quiet voice starts creeping in—*I'm grinding but getting nowhere. Am I actually growing? Why should I keep pushing forward?*

When growth feels invisible, the story turns inward and often downward. But when it's named—seen, valued, and celebrated—everything begins to shift. Momentum builds. A sense of self-efficacy takes root: *I can handle this. I can lead through this.* And joy begins to return—not just at the destination but during the journey itself.

Celebration isn't about ego. It's about reinforcing meaning. Every acknowledgment strengthens the identity shift underway: *I am becoming a more masterful, authentic leader.* Timely reflection builds resilience. When progress—especially value-aligned progress—is noticed, it boosts the internal motivation to keep going. This works because of how we're wired.

Research in neuroscience and behavioral psychology shows that when a stretch effort is followed by meaningful acknowledgment—whether internal or external—it increases the likelihood the behavior will be repeated.[52] Recognition reinforces learning. It helps us associate growth with something that feels worthwhile. And over time, that encouragement builds resilience. It makes the hard work of change feel worth it.

---

52   Wolfram Schultz, "Behavioral Theories and the Neurophysiology of Reward," *Annual Review of Psychology* 57 (2006): 87–115.

It also speaks to our deeper needs. As human beings, we're driven by more than outcomes—we want to feel capable, connected, and purposeful. When leaders feel competent in their role and are recognized by others, their energy to keep going increases. They're more likely to stay engaged, curious, and committed to their own growth.

And over time, something deeper starts to take shape: Identity begins to shift. With each moment of recognition, the journeyman starts to internalize the change. They are no longer just thinking, *I'm acting like a leader.* They start thinking, *I am a leader. This is who I am now.* That's why it matters to recognize not only what gets done but what transforms along the way.

Leadership milestones aren't just about outcomes; they are meaningful markers of evolution: threshold moments, turning points, expansion points. Times when a leader steps into a new level of capacity, or something inside them quietly shifts. They reflect a change in mindset, presence, influence, or resilience that brings the leader closer to who they're becoming.

Some milestones are visible—such as resolving conflict with empathy, aligning a team, or leading an initiative that moves the needle. Others happen beneath the surface: choosing courage over comfort, letting go of the need to control, trusting intuition over fear, or standing alone in support of a values-based decision. These are the moments that shape identity. They may not show up on dashboards, but they're real—and they're hard.

To begin to recognize them, leaders can start by asking themselves these questions:

- *What shifted in me through this experience?*

- *How did I lead differently from how I would have before?*

The most meaningful growth often lives in micromoments: subtle acts of clarity, restraint, creativity, or emotional presence. And often, others notice our shifts before we do. A colleague's simple reflection—"You handled that with so much more presence than a year ago"—can hold up a mirror we didn't know we needed. Feedback from trusted peers and mentors matters because growth seen by others becomes harder to dismiss. When feedback is specific, timely, and grounded in values, it reinforces identity and encourages repeated behavior.

A Vistage member I worked with created a simple practice that brought this to life: a stack of twenty-five-dollar gift cards at the front desk. Any employee could give one to a peer—but only when they witnessed someone living the company's values: initiative, ownership, accountability. And it had to be public. For instance, "I'm giving this to Jordan because he stayed late to help me troubleshoot a client issue—that's what ownership looks like here." It wasn't about favoritism. It was about reinforcing fundamentals.

A Vistage speaker I admire teaches companies to define their core values not as vague ideals but as clearly articulated behaviors. *Integrity means this. Initiative looks like that.* That's what this member was reinforcing. The gift cards weren't just rewards—they were culture in action. Some leaders build quiet rituals for acknowledgment: a personal journal, a bell rung in a meeting, a handwritten note. These rituals become touchpoints—tools for making meaning that tether performance to identity and help leaders and teams remember who they are becoming.

THE INNER WORK OF RECOGNITION

Sometimes, recognizing growth starts with something as simple as pausing after a hard meeting and asking, *What changed in me?* Other times, you need someone else to help you see it. A mentor's reflection can reveal a shift you don't yet have words for. That was true for me.

Like many high-performing leaders, I didn't always notice my own growth—especially in the early years. If it wasn't dramatic, I dismissed it. I gave credit only to the big wins. I never paused to see the small, incremental gains—such as how hard it was, at first, just to let go of control.

When I first started delegating, it scared me. *What if they screwed it up? What if it costs me credibility or results?* I had to get an executive coach to walk me through it. She helped me slow down, pick one person, and just try. Not the whole department—just one place. That was the beginning of deliberate practice, specifically of delegation and building capacity through one-to-ones, though I didn't have that language yet.

Back then, I had a habit of spotting what wasn't working. What I didn't have was the ability to see what was. My coach helped me shift that lens to notice effort, intent, and progress. It changed everything. That first person I chose to focus my practice on figured it out, and I started trying it elsewhere.

And life got easier. I didn't name the win at the time—I just felt a sense of relief. It wasn't until years later, during my leadership certification work, that I saw myself in the frameworks. I recognized my old reactive patterns and finally had language to describe what had shifted in me. That helped me teach it to others.

The same was true with vulnerability. That was the hardest thing I've ever had to learn. I didn't grow up in a world where being seen felt safe. Sharing how I felt or why something mattered felt risky. I had to practice it deliberately. A coach helped me start small: one moment of honesty at a time. I'd explain why something was important to me. And slowly, I saw that people didn't turn away. They leaned in. They understood. I became more human in their eyes—not less capable but more connected.

That's what it means to celebrate the work in progress. To see leadership not as a string of perfect moves but as a long arc of deliberate, imperfect effort. And to be just realistic—and compassionate—enough to notice when something's shifting for the better.

Still, many leaders struggle to acknowledge their own growth. Imposter syndrome shows up in almost every leader I work with—sometimes quietly, sometimes in full force. It's that inner voice that says, *Who am I to be in this role? What if I'm not really the one who should be doing this?*

Especially when someone is stepping into a new level of leadership, that doubt can creep in. But here's what I've come to believe: That feeling isn't a flaw. It's a sign that you care. You're not sure if you're up to it—because the stakes are real, and you know it. The problem isn't the doubt. The problem is when you let the doubt run you. Do you have self-doubt, or does self-doubt have you?

What's helped me—and many of my clients—is learning to relate to that inner voice with some perspective. Your self-doubt isn't the enemy. It's a protective part of you that formed early and once served a purpose. Leave it unexamined and it can take over. But with awareness, you can thank it for its service and move on. That's an example of nonjudgmental awareness—instead of labeling the doubt as *bad*, you can simply notice it. You don't have to argue with it or shove it down. Just see it clearly—and keep walking.

And that brings us back to the reality that leaders shouldn't walk alone. Whether it's a coach, a peer group, or a trusted advisor, we all need people who can remind us who we really are—especially when our own minds get cloudy. People who can say, "You're not faking it. You're growing into it." That kind of reflection is not only comforting but also clarifying.

Self-doubt doesn't disqualify you from leadership. If anything, it means you're paying attention. Mastery isn't the absence of doubt. It's the ability to walk forward with it—and keep showing up anyway.

CELEBRATING COLLECTIVE GROWTH

Leadership also means encouraging and recognizing growth in others—especially within your team. In those cases, celebration isn't just a nice-to-have. It's a cultural act. It anchors meaning, reinforces identity, and builds the emotional foundation for future performance.

A well-timed acknowledgment can do more than mark an achievement. It creates a shared emotional memory—*We did this together.* It communicates that effort matters, that contribution is seen, and that values are alive in the day-to-day, not just printed on the wall. These moments deepen trust. They build psychological safety. They quietly say, *You belong here. What you do makes a difference.*

Feedback plays a key role in this. Done well, it's not just information—it's transformation. When feedback is specific, behavior-based, and delivered close to the moment, it accelerates learning, strengthens confidence, and deepens trust. People connect their actions to outcomes. They internalize the message: *I can influence what happens here.* That builds self-efficacy, especially for emerging leaders navigating new levels of complexity.

The timing matters. To really land, I believe feedback should be delivered within forty-eight hours. If too much time passes, the connection between behavior and impact fades. But when you catch someone within a day or two—"I saw the way you restructured that kickoff meeting. You made space for input, and we uncovered two major risks before they could trip us up"—the effect is lasting.

It's not simply praise. It's a mirror. And it shows people they're growing in ways that matter. More importantly, feedback helps shape identity. When people see how their actions created a real result, they begin to internalize the message: *This is who I'm becoming. This is how I lead here.*

I've worked with leaders who've built entire cultures around this kind of practice. One team rang a bell every time someone made a decision that aligned with their core values. Another kept a handwritten journal in which each team member could note something they saw a colleague do well. These weren't meaningless pizza parties; they were cultural anchors—visible, repeatable signals that said: *We notice. We value growth. And we're in this together.*

And by "together," I mean everyone, not just the most visible players. Good leaders recognize the behind-the-scenes work too. The person who asked a hard question that shifted the strategy. The one who stayed late to make sure the deck was clean.

These moments matter because they reinforce a shared story: *We are a team that shows up. That leads. That grows together.* Leadership means shaping culture, and culture is shaped in moments—small, specific, real-time acknowledgments that say: *What you did mattered. Who you're becoming matters more.*

Celebration, done well, dignifies the past, energizes the present, and invites the future. For the leadership journeyman—who is constantly experimenting, stretching, and adjusting—these feedback moments provide vital course correction. Without them, it's easy to fall back into old habits—or to hesitate. But with clear, timely recognition, the journey forward becomes clearer. The path feels real. And the motivation to keep growing strengthens.

So ask yourself these questions:

- *Are we celebrating progress in ways that reinforce our culture and values?*

- *Who showed up behind the scenes—and do they know it mattered?*

- *What story do we want this milestone to tell about who we are becoming?*

Because in the end, it's not just about acknowledging success. It's about building belief—individually and collectively—that we're capable of becoming even more.

SUSTAINING THE SPIRIT OF CELEBRATION

Sometimes the celebration is loud. Sometimes it's quiet. Reflection can be one of the most powerful ways to mark the path. It gives shape to the journey. It slows us down just enough to notice the inner work we've done—the small shifts in how we respond, listen, decide, or lead. Reflection turns experience into insight, and insight into capacity. It helps us recognize the wisdom that's already accumulating—often quietly, beneath the surface. It also orients us forward—with more clarity, more gratitude, and greater self-trust. That's what makes it so essential for leaders. It's not just a review—it's a compass.

One of the mindsets I return to often is this: The path is made meaningful not only by the peaks we reach but by the way we witness and honor each step taken along the way.

When leaders pause to reflect, even briefly, powerful questions emerge:

- *If I could celebrate just one thing about my leadership this season, what would it be?*

- *What invisible victories deserve acknowledgment?*

- *What story am I telling myself about this journey—and how might I choose to tell it as a story of courage and growth?*

Some of the biggest breakthroughs I've had didn't come in the moment. They came later—on the drive home after a tough conversation or a breakthrough coaching session, when the noise had faded and I could ask myself: *What just happened? What did I learn? How did I show up differently?*

That kind of debrief became a habit. A quiet ritual. And over time, it shaped how I saw myself. At first, a coach helped guide that process—someone who believed in me and helped me notice what was working, not just what wasn't. But eventually, I developed the capacity to do it on my own. That's what reflection builds: not just insight but self-trust.

Celebration isn't just about moments—it's a mindset. And when it becomes part of the culture, it's a force multiplier. Leaders who prioritize intentional, value-based recognition help shape how others experience meaning, progress, and belonging at work. That doesn't mean constant applause. It means regular, grounded reinforcement of the real effort people are making—visible and invisible. It means creating systems that honor the journey, not just the finish line.

Which brings us back, again, to deliberate practice—structured, intentional effort aimed at growth. It belongs here, in a chapter about celebration, because deliberate practice is hard. It asks leaders to stretch into discomfort, try new behaviors, risk failure in pursuit of something better.

Without acknowledgment—moments of recognition that say this effort matters—that kind of work can feel thankless. Progress becomes invisible. The stretch begins to feel like strain. Celebration gives shape to the process. It turns all that behind-the-scenes effort into something seen, named, and valued.

The key is consistency, not duration. You choose something to practice, engage with it intentionally, and then reflect on what happened. Every day. And when you do that? That alone is worth celebrating. Even if you're awkward. Even if you fall short. Just the fact that you tried—that you stepped into something uncomfortable with the intent to learn—that's the milestone.

That's what moves people from reactive to creative. From competent to masterful. That's also a place where a coach or peer group can help. They can help you notice patterns you can't see, reflect on what you're learning, and remind you what matters. But the decision to show up for that twenty minutes each day? That's yours. And if you can do that—and celebrate it, even quietly—you're doing the work.

One of the most vivid images I've ever seen of this kind of celebration came on my last day in Santiago. I was sitting in a café I'd visited every morning since finishing the Camino. A few tables over sat a woman in a beautifully pleated gown—formal, elegant, perfectly pressed. Her hands showed signs of rheumatoid arthritis with swollen, twisted fingers. She moved slowly, sipping her coffee with quiet joy.

She told me she had walked the final seventy-five miles from Astorga—the minimum required to receive the completion certificate. Ten miles a day, no more. But she did it. And what struck me most was the care she had taken—the dress she had carried, the dignity she brought to the moment. She was celebrating quietly, yet fully. With grace.

That's what this whole chapter has been about. Marking progress. Honoring growth. And remembering that mastery isn't a finish line. It's an ongoing relationship—with the work, the self, and the road ahead.

REFLECTION QUESTIONS/EXERCISES

1. Where do I tend to diminish or dismiss my own progress—and how might I honor it instead?

2. If I could celebrate just one thing about my leadership this season, what would it be?

3. What invisible victories have I earned lately—the ones no one saw but that still changed me?

4. What does true, soulful celebration look like for me on this path—not performative, not polished, but real?

5. What story am I telling myself about my leadership journey—and how could I reframe it as a story of courage, resilience, and growth?

In our next and final chapter, we'll explore what comes after the milestone—when growth is no longer the goal but a byproduct of purpose. Because, for the leadership journeyman, the journey doesn't end at Santiago; it continues with new eyes, deeper intention, and a different question: *Growth for what purpose?*

THE NEXT CAMINO

I honor those who rid themselves of every false self,
who empty themselves and become only clear being.

—RUMI

If you've made it here, you've already started something.

This hasn't been a book of answers. It's been a walking companion. An invitation to let go of fixed identities, take an honest look in the mirror, and step forward with greater awareness. Because the real work of leadership—the real Camino—doesn't end when you close this book.

It continues.

Growth isn't a finish line. It's a way of traveling. And the leaders who stay in the work are the ones who keep walking—not because they're trying to fix themselves but because they've made peace with the fact that the journey never ends.

So as the road bends again, the question that lives here is the one I find myself asking most often:

> *Growth for what purpose?*

It comes up more than you'd think. There's a baked-in assumption in most companies that they're supposed to grow—top line, bottom line, head count, market share. And I get it. That's the societal pressure. That's what *The Wall Street Journal* says. That's what gets rewarded.

But it's not always good. In fact, for some people, it's horrible. The juice just isn't worth the squeeze. And they don't realize it until they've squeezed everything else out of their lives. So when someone tells me they want to grow, I get curious:

Why?

What's driving that desire?

What's the story underneath it?

Because if a $10 million company is where you're going to feel the most joy, then forget the $1 billion benchmark. Run a $10 million company brilliantly. That's not playing small—that's playing in alignment.

One of the Vistage members I've worked with over the years came to that exact place. She's not chasing a $50 million company. She's running an $8–$10 million company with her husband. She's built a culture she believes in. She still touches the customer. She reinvents her business every time the market shifts—five times and counting. And she's doing meaningful work in a way that lets her have a meaningful life.

That's growth, too.

Sometimes, the most powerful thing I can offer a leader is permission.

Permission to stop carrying the weight of someone else's expectations.

Permission to lead a great company, not a bigger one.

Permission to decide what success actually means—for them.

And when that lands—when they really get that—it's like watching someone exhale for the first time in years.

So again, I'll ask the question:

> *What is this growth for?*

It's for the moment when your presence creates safety in a room full of tension.

It's for the moment your team faces chaos and doesn't look to you for answers—they look to each other.

It's for the moment you realize that what you're building isn't just a business; it's a vessel for meaning, for people you care about, for work that matters.

It's for becoming the kind of leader whose growth makes room for everyone else to grow.

For me, the answer keeps unfolding. The longer I walk this path, the more I realize growth isn't about adding something new. It's about uncovering what's already there. It's about paying closer attention. Listening more deeply. Meeting the moment with just a little more honesty and a little less resistance.

The Camino broke me open. Not in a tragic way. In a sacred way.

There's a line from Rumi I've always loved: *The cracks are where the light gets in.* But what I've come to understand is that the cracks also let something out. They reveal what's essential. What's been waiting—your divine light to emerge as an offering to the world.

What I'm more aware of now is how and when I close myself off. When I shrink. When I grip too tightly. The Camino didn't just teach me where I was going. It taught me how to walk.

And the walk hasn't ended. There's always the next Camino. The next stretch of road. The next opportunity to bring more of myself to the surface. Not more in the sense of effort—but more in the sense of presence. More in the sense of wholeness.

For me, that next Camino looks like continuing my Vistage work, walking through whatever doors this book opens, and embracing this chapter of life with my wife, my son, my friends, and the leaders I walk beside. But more than anything, it means continuing to emerge—unconstricted and unconstrained—into the situations that ask for all of me. Not just the expert, not just the coach, but the human. The whole presence.

> *There are those who give and know not pain in giving nor do they seek joy, nor give with mindfulness of virtue ... They give as in yonder valley the myrtle breathes its fragrance into space.*
>
> **—KAHLIL GIBRAN**

That's the path now. To give that way. Not from striving, not from effort, not even from intention—but from presence. From the accumulated shape of a life lived with attention and a heart that stays open to the work.

That's what brings me to my fourth and final Camino revelation.

WABI-SABI: THE BEAUTY IN THE CRACKS

If you remember the beginning of this journey—standing at the Cruz de Ferro, laying my rock down, walking into that pilgrim hotel, and catching my reflection in the mirror—then you'll understand where this came from. That face I saw staring back at me—tired, lined, worn down—stopped me in my tracks.

It wasn't a breakdown. It was a recognition. I didn't have words for it then, but what I came to understand in the days and miles that followed was this: I had been spending a lot of my life trying to outrun that moment. Trying to be perfect. Trying to prove I was still sharp, still strong, still relevant. Trying to hold things together—my body, my business, my identity—as if I could somehow make them permanent.

But I couldn't. And I don't need to.

THE WISDOM OF WABI-SABI

Wabi-sabi is a Japanese aesthetic and worldview that embraces imperfection, impermanence, and incompleteness. It finds beauty not in what is flawless or polished but in what has been shaped by time, weathered by life, and worn into authenticity. It's the crack in the pottery that's been handed down for generations. The weathered wood that tells a story. The wrinkle in a face that's earned its wisdom.

Wabi-sabi doesn't say "fix it"—it says "see it." It asks us to value what's real, not what's ideal. And in leadership, that's a radical act. Because we've been taught to present the polished version of ourselves. But soulful leadership calls for something else: the courage to lead with the cracks visible. Not because we're broken but because we're becoming.

Wabi-sabi is the truth that finally gave shape to what I was learning on that walk.

PRESENCE-LED LEADERSHIP

The leadership journeyman doesn't lead from perfection. We lead from presence. From the wisdom that comes not in spite of the hard parts but because of them. From the ability to walk with what's unfinished and still keep going.

I'm not here to be perfect. I'm not here to be permanent. I'm not here to be complete.

That was the mirror.

This is the meaning.

These days, I find myself traveling lighter. I speak less. I listen longer. I lead with less armor. What matters most to me now isn't polish—it's clarity. Soulful clarity. The kind that comes from having walked far enough to know there's no final version of me to get to.

The journey never ends.

The beauty is in the becoming.

WHAT COMES NEXT

The Camino never really ends. There's always another stretch of road—another layer of the work. For me, that next stretch is subtle. It's less about learning new frameworks and more about letting go of whatever's still in the way. Less about doing. More about being.

This past year, I've been leaning into something new. I've been studying with Bob Anderson through the Unity Academy—a program that brings together leadership, quantum physics, and energetic presence.

That may sound abstract, but to me, it's become incredibly practical. It's given language to something I've felt for a long time: Leadership is less about what you do and more about how you show up. Not as a persona. Not as a title. But as a presence. As energy in the room.

That's my next frontier. To become less constrained. Less constricted. To show up as myself—without filter, without performance. To be, in every moment, fully present and fully available to the people in front of me.

My goal is simple, and it's audacious:

To be a vessel of divine grace.

If I can do that—if I can bring that kind of presence into a conversation with a client, or a moment with my wife, or a dinner with my son—then they're getting the very best of me. And that's enough.

That's a good life. An ordinary life well lived.

I'm not here to invent the cure for cancer. I'm just going to show up and do my thing. Let the years I've lived—the work I've done, the cracks I've earned, the wisdom I've gathered—breathe their fragrance into the space I'm in.

I wouldn't be here without the people I've walked beside. The members I've coached, the leaders I've served, the Vistage community I've been part of for over two decades—they've grown me up in ways I couldn't have imagined. That's the real privilege. That's the gift I carry forward.

That's my next Camino.

And now the question becomes: *What's yours?*

THE JOURNEY CONTINUES

Where is your next stretch? What's the threshold you're standing at—and are you ready to cross it?

Maybe it's in your business. Maybe it's in how you lead. Maybe it's something internal you've been avoiding for a while. Wherever it is, it starts the same way: Decide. Simply decide that you are a person who grows. Then get curious about where.

The leadership journeyman doesn't wait for certainty. We walk forward without all the answers. We commit first—then the road shows up. Courage doesn't mean we're not afraid. It just means we walk with fear instead of waiting for it to leave. We trust that what's ahead will meet us.

And curiosity? That's how we lead when control isn't possible:

What might be possible here?

What if this challenge is an invitation?

Curiosity is the antidote to fear—and the beginning of transformation.

When you lead that way, others follow. You give your team permission to bring their full selves. Innovation rises. Authenticity spreads. People stop fearing the unknown—and start cocreating within it.

Leaders who walk into the fog with open eyes become the light for others. And here's the truth: You don't have to walk alone. If there's one thing I've learned from two decades of coaching CEOs, it's that the work is too complex—and too important—to do in isolation. The most powerful growth I've seen doesn't come from having the right answers. It comes from being in the right room. From being with people who will challenge your assumptions, hold you accountable, and remind you who you are when you forget.

That's the value of a great peer group—whether it's the Young Presidents' Organization, Entrepreneurs' Organization, Women Presidents Organization, Convene, Chief, or any high-integrity circle of leaders committed to deep, real growth. These groups provide more than perspective—they provide a mirror. A cadence of clarity. A culture of accountability. A place where you can think out loud, surface blind spots, and walk away with better decisions—which you made faster and more confidently. Not because someone handed them to you but because you earned them in conversation with people who are walking the same road.

As a Vistage Chair with Vistage Worldwide, I've seen this power up close. The Vistage groups I lead are a place to grow—not just professionally but personally. I know because I've seen firsthand that when leaders commit to real growth, they don't just scale their businesses. They become better thinkers. Better parents. Better partners.

That growth doesn't stay in the boardroom. It moves through every part of their lives.

Vistage isn't a class or a workshop. It's a circle of peers who witness your journey—and keep you honest in your walk. I can do a lot as a coach. But I've never done more for a leader than what a high-performing peer group can do for each other. So if you're looking for your next stretch—if you're standing at the edge of your own threshold space—find your people. Find the circle that will hold you steady and push you forward.

I remember standing in the courtyard at Santiago, surrounded by pilgrims celebrating their arrival, and realizing: This isn't the end.

There will be another Camino.

This book is one of them.

So is whatever comes next.

Begin it now.

I've shared many stories in these pages—mine, and those of the leaders I've walked beside. But in the end, all of this work is about one thing: choosing "to love fiercely the life, the work, the leadership that is rightfully yours."

That idea comes from a poem that has shaped me for years. It's called *The Truelove,* by David Whyte, and it captures something essential about the moment when we stop waiting and start living. When we recognize the truth that's been calling to us all along.

In live readings and workshops, David has been known to play with the opening line—replacing "the one who is rightfully yours" with "the life," "the self," or "the path." In that spirit, and with full respect to his original, I offer a version that speaks most deeply to the work of this book:

> *There's a faith in loving fiercely the leader that you rightfully are ...*

And from there, I leave you with the poem as he wrote it.

The Truelove
David Whyte, The House of Belonging[53]

There is a faith in loving fiercely

the one who is rightfully yours,

especially if you have

waited years and especially

if part of you never believed

you could deserve this

loved and beckoning hand

held out to you this way.

I am thinking of faith now

and the testaments of loneliness

and what we feel we are

worthy of in this world.

Years ago in the Hebrides

I remember an old man

who walked every morning

on the grey stones

to the shore of the baying seals,

who would press his hat

to his chest in the blustering

salt wind and say his prayer

to the turbulent Jesus

hidden in the water,

and I think of the story

---

53 David Whyte, "The Truelove," in *The House of Belonging* (Many Rivers Press, 1996), 15.

of the storm and everyone

waking and seeing

the distant

yet familiar figure

far across the water

calling to them,

and how we are all

preparing for that

abrupt waking,

and that calling,

and that moment

we have to say yes,

except it will

not come so grandly,

so Biblically,

but more subtly

and intimately in the face

of the one you know

you have to love,

so that when we finally step out of the boat

toward them, we find

everything holds

us, and confirms

our courage, and if you wanted

to drown you could,

but you don't

because finally

after all the struggle

and all the years,

you don't want to any more,

you've simply had enough
of drowning
and you want to live and you
want to love and you will
walk across any territory
and any darkness,
however fluid and however
dangerous, to take the
one hand you know
belongs in yours.

ONE FINAL NOTE
(For those ready to take the next step.)

If you've read this far, thank you. That tells me something about you. You're not just interested in leadership—you're committed to growth. You're already on the Camino.

If something in this book stirred something in you—an insight, a question, a quiet *yes*—then I want to invite you to stay in the conversation. You can do one or all of the following:

- Explore joining a Vistage peer group.

- Take the Leadership Circle Profile 360-degree assessment that I mentioned at the beginning of the book. If you missed it there, here's the QR code to opt in:

- Or simply reach out and connect with me here:

This work is ongoing. This journey is better when it's shared.

Wherever your next threshold is, I hope you cross it with curiosity, with courage, and with company.

See you on the trail.

—Peter

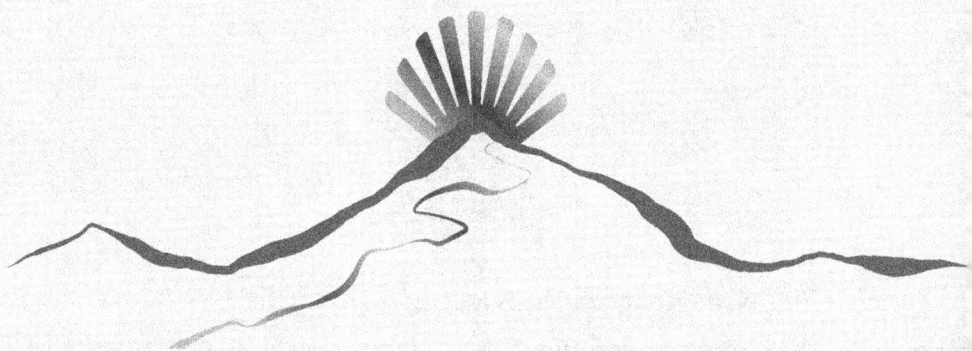

ACKNOWLEDGMENTS

A heartfelt thank you to every Vistage member and CEO client I have worked with these past twenty years. You are truly the heroes of the US economy. The greatest privilege of my professional life is being a witness to everything you do to grow your businesses and take care of your employees.

A heartfelt thank you to Vistage Worldwide, the amazing support center, and especially the support of Lee Peters and Sam Reese. Lee, your leadership presence has been an absolute joy to work with in my role as Best Practice Chair. Sam, I have benefited enormously from your leadership and vision for Vistage Worldwide these past several years. I cherish the personal connection I enjoy with both Lee and you. Thank you!

To my fellow Vistage Chairs, particularly the Washington, DC, community, thank you for your generous spirits. I have grown so much as a Chair and a man because of many of you.

A heartfelt thank you to all the teachers and mentors I referenced in the book. I have so much respect and admiration for your contributions to the field of leadership development.

Thank you to the "Thursday morning men's group" I belonged to for many years. It was my first peer group experience. It was powerful and transformative. I am very grateful for that experience, gentlemen.

My family: Thank you, Mom and Dad. Thank you, Tom, Donna, and Cathy—I am fortunate to have you as my brother and sisters. I love you very much.

And finally, my greatest heartfelt appreciation and gratitude . . . my wife Elaine, your love, support, and belief in me matters more than you know. My son, Peter Reza. Thank you. Those Saturday morning conversations were invaluable in helping me gather my thoughts as I wrote this book. You are on a noble path. I love your dedication, discipline, and passion for your own journey.

ABOUT THE AUTHOR

PETER SCHWARTZ is an award-winning CEO coach, author, and leadership consultant who guides leaders on transformative journeys, mastering the "inner and outer games" of leadership effectiveness. Leveraging a thirty-year career in telecom including owning his own business, Peter became a Vistage Chair with Vistage Worldwide in 2005. Recognized internationally for his leadership impact, Peter was named a Vistage Best Practice Chair in 2013. He has won several awards, including the Robert Nourse Vistage Chair of the Year in 2016 and the prestigious Don Cope memorial award—the highest honor for a Vistage Chair—in 2020.

Dedicated to fostering authentic dialogue, Peter helps CEOs and senior executive teams cut through complexity, clarify their purpose, and lead with conviction. His nuanced approach to leadership development draws from adult development theory, The Leadership Circle, and neuroscience, combining deep insight with actionable strategies leaders can apply across any industry.

Peter's new book, *The Leadership Journeyman*, captures his passion for developing purpose-driven leaders who leave lasting legacies, empowering them to embrace their journey with courage, curiosity, and a profound sense of possibility.

www.ingramcontent.com/pod-product-compliance
Lightning Source LLC
Jackson TN
JSHW022353241025
92995JS00003BA/4

9798897010387